BASKETBALL
TOP 10

BASKETBALL TOP 10

BY JOHN HAREAS

DK PUBLISHING INC

CONTENTS

LONDON, NEW YORK, MELBOURNE, MUNICH, and DELHI

Project Editor Anja Schmidt
Designer Megan Clayton
DTP Milos Orlovic
Production Manager Chris Avgherinos
Creative Director Tina Vaughan
Project Director Sharon Lucas
Publisher Chuck Lang

NBA Publishing Charles Rosenzweig, Mario Argote,
Michael Levine, David Mintz, Margaret Williams
NBA Entertainment Photos Carmin Romanelli, Joe Amati,
David Bonilla, Pam Costello, John Kristofick,
Bennett Renda, Brian Choi, Scott Yurdin
NBA Entertainment Adam Silver, Gregg Winik, Paul Hirschheimer,
Marc Hirschheimer, Rob Sario, Tony Stewart
Photo Editor Joe Amati
Writer John Hareas
NBA Staff Photographers Andrew D. Bernstein,
Nathaniel S. Butler, Jesse D. Garrabrant

For more statistical fun log onto

www.nba.com

Published in the United States in 2004 by DK Publishing, Inc.,
375 Hudson Street, New York, New York 10014

06 07 08 09 10 2 4 6 8 10 9 7 5 3

Copyright © 2004 DK Publishing, Inc. and NBA Properties, Inc.

ISBN-13: 978-0-7566-0321-2
ISBN-10: 0-7566-0321-8

Reproduced by Colourscan, Singapore
Printed and bound in China by Toppan

Discover more at

www.dk.com

Steve Nash

George Mikan

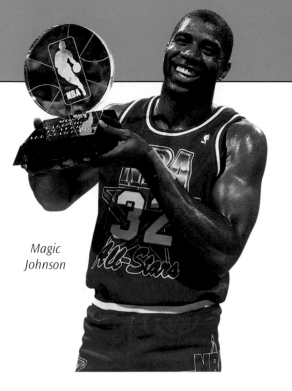

Magic Johnson

TOP 10

TEAM BY TEAM

NBA FINALS

NBA PLAYOFFS

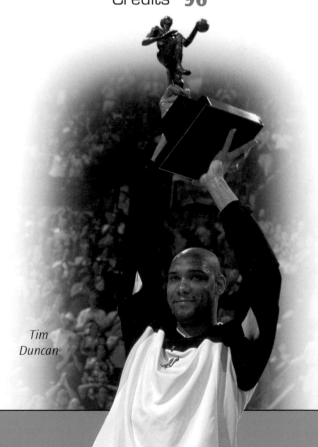

Tim Duncan

Who are the top 10 scorers in NBA history? Who has dished the most assists in a single game? Who is the Philadelphia 76ers all-time leading scorer with 21,586 points? Wilt Chamberlain? Julius Erving? Charles Barkley? Try Hal Greer. Did you know that the shortest player in NBA history, Muggsy Bogues, is 5-3 and enjoyed a 14-year career? Or that Hakeem Olajuwon leads all international players with 26,946 points?

In 1891, Dr. James Naismith invented the game of basketball to keep rowdy students at the International YMCA Training School in Springfield, Massachusetts, busy during the winter months. Before long, the game was being played in YMCAs across the country, and barnstorming leagues began popping up along the East Coast. In the 1940s, arena owners started a league to fill their calendars, and this league became the National Basketball Association in 1946.

Phil Jackson and the Chicago Bulls celebrate another championship win.

Throughout the 57-year history of the NBA, nearly 4,000 players have logged at least one minute of action, yet only an exclusive group is featured in the pages of this book. Legendary players such as George Mikan, Bill Russell, Wilt Chamberlain, Kareem Abdul-Jabbar, Magic Johnson, Larry Bird, and Michael Jordan are joined by some of today's brightest stars—Shaquille O'Neal, Allen Iverson, and Tim Duncan—in elevating basketball greatness to a higher form.

Basketball Top 10 goes beyond the numbers. You'll learn a myriad of facts, from the Top 10 tallest players in NBA history to what country has contributed the most talent to this global game, from what coach has the most championship rings to which team has had the most players inducted into the Naismith Memorial Basketball Hall of Fame. You'll even read about which team lost a coin flip to draft a young basketball superstar named Magic Johnson.

What are you waiting for? A wealth of basketball fun and information is only a page away. Enjoy!

* indicates players, coaches, or teams that have retired or folded prior to the 2003–04 season

Reggie Miller shoots over Paul Pierce.

TEAM IDENTIFIERS (used throughout the book)

The identifiers below correspond to the city or state that the team has played or currently plays in.

ATL	Atlanta Hawks	**IND**	Indiana Pacers	**PHI**	Philadelphia 76ers
BOS	Boston Celtics	**KC**	Kansas City Kings	**PHO**	Phoenix Suns
BUF	Buffalo Braves	**LAC**	Los Angeles Clippers	**POR**	Portland Trail Blazers
CHA	Charlotte Hornets	**LAL**	Los Angeles Lakers	**SAC**	Sacramento Kings
CHI	Chicago Bulls	**MEM**	Memphis Grizzlies	**SAN**	San Antonio Spurs
CIN	Cincinnati Royals	**MIA**	Miami Heat	**SF**	San Francisco Warriors
CLE	Cleveland Cavaliers	**MIL**	Milwaukee Bucks	**SEA**	Seattle SuperSonics
DAL	Dallas Mavericks	**MIN**	Minnesota Timberwolves	**SYR**	Syracuse Nationals
DEN	Denver Nuggets	**NJ**	New Jersey Nets	**TOR**	Toronto Raptors
DET	Detroit Pistons	**NO**	New Orleans Jazz	**UT**	Utah Jazz
GS	Golden State Warriors	**NY**	New York Knicks	**WAS**	Washington Wizards
HOU	Houston Rockets	**ORL**	Orlando Magic		

REGULAR SEASON

FLYING HIGH

During his 15 years as a player in the NBA, Michael Jordan rose to the top of many NBA regular-season records. From most scoring titles to the highest career scoring average in NBA history, Jordan left an indelible mark on the game.

THE TOP 10

Most NBA MVPs

PLAYER	AWARDS
1 Kareem Abdul-Jabbar*	6
2 =Michael Jordan*	5
=Bill Russell*	5
4 Wilt Chamberlain*	4
5 =Larry Bird*	3
=Magic Johnson*	3
=Moses Malone*	3
8 =Tim Duncan	2
=Karl Malone	2
=Bob Pettit*	2

MR. MVP

The résumé sparkles in achievement. In 15 NBA seasons, Michael Jordan has assembled quite a trophy collection. The 6-6 shooting guard won five NBA MVP awards and six NBA Finals MVP awards along with a long list of numerous other honors.

THE TOP 10

Most NBA Finals MVPs

PLAYER	AWARDS
1 Michael Jordan*	6
2 =Magic Johnson*	3
=Shaquille O'Neal	3
4 =Kareem Abdul-Jabbar*	2
=Larry Bird*	2
=Tim Duncan	2
=Hakeem Olajuwon*	2
=Willis Reed*	2
9 =Rick Barry*	1
=Wilt Chamberlain*	1
=Joe Dumars*	1
=John Havlicek*	1
=Dennis Johnson*	1
=Moses Malone*	1
=Cedric Maxwell*	1
=Isiah Thomas*	1
=Wes Unseld*	1
=Bill Walton*	1
=Jo Jo White*	1
=James Worthy*	1

The NBA MVP award was first introduced in 1969, and Jerry West of the Los Angeles Lakers was the first recipient. Since then, some of the NBA's greatest players have taken home one of sport's most prestigious honors. Michael Jordan is a perfect six for six, having led the Chicago Bulls to six NBA championships in eight years.

ELITE COMPANY

In his first five seasons, Tim Duncan has already established himself as one of the NBA's greatest players ever. The Spurs' All-Star won back-to-back NBA MVP awards. Only six other players in NBA history have won the award in consecutive seasons.

THE TOP 10

Most Defensive Player of the Year Awards

PLAYER	AWARDS
1 Dikembe Mutombo	4
2 =Mark Eaton*	2
=Sidney Moncrief*	2
=Alonzo Mourning	2
=Hakeem Olajuwon*	2
=Dennis Rodman*	2
=Ben Wallace	2
8 =Michael Cooper*	1
=Michael Jordan*	1
=Gary Payton	1
=Alvin Robertson*	1
=David Robinson*	1

The NBA Defensive Player of the Year Award was first issued following the 1982–83 season. It recognizes the player who is the most dominant defensive force in the game. Sidney Moncrief of the Milwaukee Bucks was the first recipient.

DID YOU KNOW?
Michael Jordan holds the NBA Finals single-series record for highest points-per-game average with 41.0. He reached that record versus the Phoenix Suns in the 1993 NBA Finals, which went six games.

The Top 10 Most All-NBA First-Team Selections

Player/Selections

1 Karl Malone 11 **2** =**Kareem Abdul-Jabbar*** 10; = **Elgin Baylor*** 10;
= **Bob Cousy*** 10; = **Michael Jordan*** 10;
= **Bob Pettit*** 10; = **Jerry West*** 10
8 =**Larry Bird*** 9; = **Magic Johnson*** 9;
= **Oscar Robertson*** 9

Twelve players were selected ahead of Karl Malone in the 1985 NBA Draft. Yet the 6-9 power forward finds himself atop very select company. No one has earned more All-NBA First Team selections than the perennial NBA All-Star. His 11 is quite an honor considering that the All-NBA Teams have been around as long as the NBA has existed (since 1946). A logjam exists in second place and features some of the greatest players to have ever played the game.

THE TOP 10

Most NBA Coach of the Year Awards

COACH	AWARDS
1 =**Don Nelson**	3
=**Pat Riley**	3
3 =**Bill Fitch**	2
=**Cotton Fitzsimmons**	2
=**Gene Shue**	2
6 **Many tied with**	1

The NBA Coach of the Year Award made its debut in 1963. Harry Gallatin of the St. Louis Hawks won the award after guiding his team to a 48-32 record during the 1962–63 season. Don Nelson and Pat Riley each top the list with three awards apiece. Riley won the award with three different franchises (LAL, NY, and MIA) while Nelson won with two (MIL and GS).

COACHING GREAT

Before he earned the reputation as one of the greatest NBA coaches ever, Don Nelson made a name for himself as an NBA player. As a coach, Nelson has guided the Milwaukee Bucks, Golden State Warriors, New York Knicks, and currently the Dallas Mavericks.

THE TOP 10

Last NBA MVP Winners

YEAR	PLAYER	TEAM
2003	Tim Duncan	SAN
2002	Tim Duncan	SAN
2001	Allen Iverson	PHI
2000	Shaquille O'Neal	LAL
1999	Karl Malone	UT
1998	Michael Jordan*	CHI
1997	Karl Malone	UT
1996	Michael Jordan*	CHI
1995	David Robinson*	SAN
1994	Hakeem Olajuwon*	HOU

THE TOP 10

Last NBA Rookie of the Year Winners

YEAR	PLAYER	TEAM
2003	Amare' Stoudemire	PHO
2002	Pau Gasol	MEM
2001	Mike Miller	ORL
2000	Elton Brand/Steve Francis	CHI/HOU
1999	Vince Carter	TOR
1998	Tim Duncan	SAN
1997	Allen Iverson	PHI
1996	Damon Stoudamire	TOR
1995	Grant Hill/Jason Kidd	DET/DAL
1994	Chris Webber	GS

Don Meineke of the Fort Wayne Pistons won the NBA's first Rookie of the Year award, honoring the league's top newcomer, in 1953. Two of the last 10 seasons' recipients, Allen Iverson and Tim Duncan, have gone on to win NBA MVP honors.

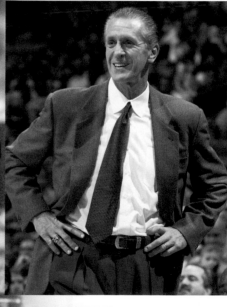

THE WINNER WITHIN

A master motivator and an excellent X's and O's tactician, Pat Riley has enjoyed tremendous success as a head coach. Riley guided the Los Angeles Lakers to four NBA championships in the 1980s, and led the New York Knicks to the 1994 NBA Finals.

THE ULTIMATE MAILMAN

For nearly 20 years, Karl Malone has delivered big results. He is on pace to eclipse Kareem Abdul-Jabbar as the league's all-time leading scorer. Abdul-Jabbar scored 38,387 points in 20 seasons while Malone has delivered 36,374 points after 18.

THE TOP 10

Highest Scoring Averages†

	PLAYER	G	FGM	FTM	PTS	AVG
1	Shaquille O'Neal	742	8,116	4,242	20,475	27.6
2	Allen Iverson	487	4,669	3,200	13,170	27.0
3	Karl Malone	1,434	13,335	9,619	36,374	25.4
4	Tim Duncan	451	3,932	2,444	10,324	22.9
5	Chris Webber	596	5,542	1,902	13,209	22.2
6	Kobe Bryant	496	3,801	2,639	10,658	21.5
7	Jerry Stackhouse	582	3,998	3,696	12,375	21.3
8	Glenn Robinson	637	5,262	2,338	13,446	21.1
9	Grant Hill	482	3,645	2,756	10,104	21.0
10	Antoine Walker	528	4,229	1,625	10,995	20.8

† 400 games or 10,000 points minimum

The Top 10 Leading Scorers

Player/Points

1 Karl Malone 36,374 **2** Reggie Miller 23,505 **3** Shaquille O'Neal 20,475 **4** Scottie Pippen 18,804 **5** Gary Payton 18,757 **6** Glen Rice 18,270 **7** Clifford Robinson 17,338 **8** Kevin Willis 16,990 **9** Shawn Kemp 15,347 **10** Latrell Sprewell 14,316

THE TOP 10

Most Field Goals

	PLAYER	FIELD GOALS
1	Karl Malone	13,335
2	Shaquille O'Neal	8,116
3	Reggie Miller	7,667
4	Gary Payton	7,513
5	Scottie Pippen	7,367
6	Kevin Willis	6,985
7	Glen Rice	6,754
8	Clifford Robinson	5,640
9	Chris Webber	5,542
10	Shawn Kemp	5,505

Although Shaquille O'Neal joined the NBA in 1993, he is already climbing the charts for most field goals made among active players. O'Neal, who owns two NBA scoring titles, has led the league in field goals five times in his career. The three-time NBA Finals MVP will undoubtedly add to his overall totals.

THE TOP 10

Highest Field-Goal Percentages†

	PLAYER	FGM	FGA	PCT
1	Shaquille O'Neal	8,116	14,072	.577
2	Dale Davis	3,305	6,166	.536
3	Alonzo Mourning	4,505	8,583	.525
4	Dikembe Mutombo	3,737	7,192	.520
5	Karl Malone	13,335	25,810	.517
6	Horace Grant	5,347	10,471	.511
7	Tim Duncan	3,932	7,715	.510
8	Anthony Mason	3,582	7,033	.509
9=	Tyrone Hill	2,831	5,638	.502
=	Rasheed Wallace	3,613	7,201	.502

† 2,000 FGM minimum

Shaquille O'Neal has led the NBA in field-goal percentage six times throughout his career, including five seasons in a row.

THE TOP 10

Most Free Throws

	PLAYER	FREE THROWS
1	Karl Malone	9,619
2	Reggie Miller	5,841
3	Shawn Kemp	4,304
4	Shaquille O'Neal	4,242
5	Jerry Stackhouse	3,696
6	Alonzo Mourning	3,582
7	Rod Strickland	3,351
8	Clifford Robinson	3,307
9	Derrick Coleman	3,274
10	Glen Rice	3,208

A testament to Karl Malone's dedication to the game may be best illustrated by his improvement at the free-throw line. As a rookie, Malone shot only .481 percent from the line but worked hard in the following seasons. Not only has he led the NBA in free-throw attempts seven times, he has also improved his average to nearly 80 percent.

FOCUSED

Ray Allen of the Seattle SuperSonics is one of the NBA's best free-throw shooters. He has shot 90 percent or better from the line twice in his career. Opposing teams think twice before fouling the NBA All-Star.

THE TOP 10

Highest Free-Throw Percentages†

	PLAYER	FTM	FTA	PCT
1	**Reggie Miller**	5,841	6,593	.886
2	**Ray Allen**	1,954	2,215	.882
3	**Terrell Brandon**	1,784	2,043	.873
4	**Allan Houston**	2,379	2,764	.861
5	**Derek Anderson**	1,435	1,668	.860
6	**Sam Cassell**	2,568	2,997	.857
7	**Dirk Nowitzki**	1,762	2,078	.848
8	**Glen Rice**	3,208	3,796	.845
9=	**Steve Smith**	2,918	3,462	.843
=	**Cuttino Mobley**	1,292	1,533	.843

† 1,200 FTM minimum

THE TOP 10

Most Three-Point Field Goals

	PLAYER	THREE-POINTERS
1	**Reggie Miller**	2,330
2	**Glen Rice**	1,554
3	**Nick Van Exel**	1,327
4	**Allan Houston**	1,187
5	**Ray Allen**	1,129
6	**Steve Smith**	1,064
7	**Wesley Person**	1,054
8	**Clifford Robinson**	989
9	**Eddie Jones**	982
10	**Walt Williams**	976

The three-point line was introduced in the NBA for the 1979–80 season, and no one has made more than Reggie Miller of the Indiana Pacers.

THE TOP 10

Highest 3-Pt. Field-Goal Percentages†

	PLAYER	3FGM	3FGA	PCT
1	**Hubert Davis**	728	1,650	.441
2	**Michael Redd**	270	617	.438
3	**Steve Nash**	569	1,361	.418
4	**Wesley Person**	1,054	2,527	.417
5	**Pat Garrity**	513	1,242	.413
6=	**Ray Allen**	1,129	2,809	.402
=	**Brent Barry**	876	2,178	.402
=	**Eric Piatkowski**	738	1,835	.402
=	**Glen Rice**	1,554	3,868	.402
=	**Michael Dickerson**	288	717	.402

† 250 3FGM minimum

MAV ON THE MARK

One of the premier point guards in the NBA, Steve Nash of the Dallas Mavericks likes to extend opposing defenses with his three-point shooting ability. The NBA All-Star opens up the Mavericks' inside game with his three-point accuracy.

N B A . C O M   F U N   F A C T

Ray Allen shares the NBA single-game record for most three-point field goals made in one half with eight. He achieved this against the Charlotte Hornets on April 14, 2002.

SPALDING

13

ACTIVE LEADERS

THE TOP 10
Most Games Played

	PLAYER	GAMES
1	Karl Malone	1,434
2	Kevin Willis	1,342
3	Charles Oakley	1,275
4	Mark Jackson	1,254
5	Reggie Miller	1,243
6	Scottie Pippen	1,155
7	Horace Grant	1,110
8	Clifford Robinson	1,097
9	Olden Polynice	1,056
10	Shawn Kemp	1,051

FOUR-TIME NBA CHAMP

Horace Grant has played a key role in helping his teams win NBA championships. The 6-10 power forward was invaluable when the Chicago Bulls won three titles in the early 1990s, and he also helped the Los Angeles Lakers win in 2001. Grant hopes to add a fifth ring to his collection in 2003–04 with the Lakers.

The Top 10 Most Minutes Played

Player/Minutes

1 **Karl Malone** 53,479 **2** **Reggie Miller** 43,260 **3** **Scottie Pippen** 40,657 **4** **Charles Oakley** 40,255 **5** **Mark Jackson** 38,544 **6** **Gary Payton** 37,943 **7** **Kevin Willis** 37,602 **8** **Horace Grant** 37,515 **8** **Clifford Robinson** 35,208 **8** **Glen Rice** 34,723

THE TOP 10
Most Offensive Rebounds

	PLAYER	OFFENSIVE REBOUNDS
1	Kevin Willis	4,064
2	Charles Oakley	3,924
3	Karl Malone	3,501
4	Horace Grant	3,388
5	Dikembe Mutombo	3,169
6	Shawn Kemp	3,026
7	Shaquille O'Neal	2,947
8	Dale Davis	2,913
9	Vlade Divac	2,727
10	Tyrone Hill	2,391

THE TOP 10
Most Defensive Rebounds

	PLAYER	DEFENSIVE REBOUNDS
1	Karl Malone	11,100
2	Charles Oakley	8,276
3	Kevin Willis	7,655
4	Dikembe Mutombo	7,301
5	Vlade Divac	6,104
6	Shaquille O'Neal	6,065
7	Horace Grant	5,822
8	Shawn Kemp	5,808
9	Scottie Pippen	5,378
10	Anthony Mason	5,367

DID YOU KNOW?
Horace Grant has a twin brother Harvey who was a forward for the Washington Bullets/Wizards, Portland Trail Blazers, and Philadelphia 76ers.

OAK TREE

Selected with the ninth overall pick in the 1985 NBA Draft out of Virginia Union, Charles Oakley certainly has defied the odds and enjoyed a long and productive NBA career. The 6-9 power forward earned the reputation as a hard-nosed competitor who specializes in defense and rebounding.

THE TOP 10
Most Assists

	PLAYER	ASSISTS
1	Mark Jackson	10,215
2	Rod Strickland	7,704
3	Gary Payton	7,590
4	Tim Hardaway	7,095
5	Jason Kidd	6,120
6	Scottie Pippen	6,085
7	Avery Johnson	5,735
8	Nick Van Exel	5,221
9	Karl Malone	5,085
10	Kenny Anderson	4,968

Los Angeles Laker Gary Payton continues his ascent on the NBA's all-time assists chart. The versatile 6-4 guard has averaged a little more than seven assists per game throughout his All-Star career.

THE TOP 10
Most Steals

	PLAYER	STEALS
1	Scottie Pippen	2,286
2	Gary Payton	2,147
3	Karl Malone	2,035
4	Mark Jackson	1,591
5	Rod Strickland	1,578
6	Kendall Gill	1,440
7	Tim Hardaway	1,428
8	Reggie Miller	1,390
9	Jason Kidd	1,380
10	Charles Oakley	1,351

Think of Reggie Miller and you think of lots of three-pointers. But did you know that the 6-7 shooting guard for the Indiana Pacers is also a master of the on-court theft?

THE TOP 10
Most Blocked Shots

	PLAYER	BLOCKS
1	Dikembe Mutombo	2,873
2	Shawn Bradley	1,982
3	Shaquille O'Neal	1,936
4	Alonzo Mourning	1,883
5	Vlade Divac	1,553
6	Elden Campbell	1,545
7	Shawn Kemp	1,279
8	Theo Ratliff	1,262
9	Clifford Robinson	1,201
10	Tim Duncan	1,129

Alonzo Mourning of the Miami Heat led the NBA in blocks in consecutive seasons, becoming one of the NBA's most intimidating players.

NOT IN MY HOUSE!

Zaire native Dikembe Mutombo is a walking human eraser, routinely rejecting opponents' shots. The 7-2 center has won the NBA's Defensive Player of the Year Award a record four times.

THE TOP 10
Most Rebounds Total

	PLAYER	REBOUNDS
1	Karl Malone	14,601
2	Charles Oakley	12,200
3	Kevin Willis	11,719
4	Dikembe Mutombo	10,470
5	Horace Grant	9,210
6	Shaquille O'Neal	9,012
7	Shawn Kemp	8,834
8	Vlade Divac	8,831
9	Dale Davis	7,642
10	Anthony Mason	7,279

For almost 20 years, Kevin Willis has averaged nearly nine rebounds a game. He reached the NBA Finals in 2003, when the Spurs won the title.

SHOOTING STARS

Leading Scorers

	PLAYER	POINTS
1	Kareem Abdul-Jabbar*	38,387
2	Karl Malone	36,374
3	Michael Jordan*	32,292
4	Wilt Chamberlain*	31,419
5	Moses Malone*	27,409
6	Elvin Hayes*	27,313
7	Hakeem Olajuwon*	26,946
8	Oscar Robertson*	26,710
9	Dominique Wilkins*	26,668
10	John Havlicek*	26,395

The Top 10 Most Field Goals

Player/Field Goals

1 Kareem Abdul-Jabbar* 15,837 **2** Karl Malone 13,335 **3** Wilt Chamberlain* 12,681 **4** Michael Jordan* 12,192 **5** Elvin Hayes* 10,976 **6** Hakeem Olajuwon* 10,749 **7** Alex English* 10,659 **8** John Havlicek* 10,513 **9** Dominique Wilkins* 9,963 **10** Patrick Ewing* 9,702

Highest Field-Goal Percentages

	PLAYER	FGM	FGA	PCT
1	Artis Gilmore*	5,732	9,570	.599
2	Mark West*	2,528	4,356	.580
3	Shaquille O'Neal	8,116	14,072	.577
4=	Steve Johnson*	2,841	4,965	.572
=	Darryl Dawkins*	3,477	6,079	.572
6	James Donaldson*	3,105	5,442	.571
7	Jeff Ruland*	2,105	3,734	.564
8	Kareem Abdul-Jabbar*	15,837	28,307	.559
9	Kevin McHale*	6,830	12,334	.554
10	Bobby Jones*	3,412	6,199	.550

Highest Scoring Averages†

	PLAYER	G	FGM	FTM	PTS	AVG
1	Michael Jordan*	1,072	12,192	7,327	32,292	30.12
2	Wilt Chamberlain*	1,045	12,681	6,057	31,419	30.07
3	Shaquille O'Neal	742	8,116	4,242	20,475	27.6
4	Elgin Baylor*	846	8,693	5,763	23,149	27.4
5=	Allen Iverson	487	4,669	3,200	13,170	27.0
=	Jerry West*	932	9,016	7,160	25,192	27.0
7	Bob Pettit*	792	7,349	6,182	20,880	26.4
8	George Gervin*	791	8,045	4,541	20,708	26.2
9	Oscar Robertson*	1,040	9,508	7,694	26,710	25.7
10	Karl Malone	1,434	13,335	9,619	36,374	25.4

† 400 games or 10,000 points minimum

SCORING KING

No one has scored more points in NBA history than Kareem Abdul-Jabbar. The 7-2 Hall-of-Fame center amassed 38,387 points in his 20-year NBA career and scored a significant number of those points with his trademark move, the sky hook (pictured).

The Top 10 Most Free Throws

Player/Free Throws

1 Karl Malone 9,619 **2** Moses Malone* 8,531 **3** Oscar Robertson* 7,694 **4** Michael Jordan* 7,327 **5** Jerry West* 7,160 **6** Dolph Schayes* 6,979 **7** Adrian Dantley* 6,832 **8** Kareem Abdul-Jabbar* 6,712 **9** Charles Barkley* 6,349 **10** Bob Pettit* 6,182

THE TOP 10
Highest Free-Throw Percentages†

	PLAYER	FTM	FTA	PCT
1	Mark Price*	2,135	2,362	.904
2	Rick Barry*	3,818	4,243	.900
3	Calvin Murphy*	3,445	3,864	.892
4	Scott Skiles*	1,548	1,741	.889
5=	Larry Bird*	3,960	4,471	.886
=	Reggie Miller	5,841	6,593	.886
7	Bill Sharman*	3,143	3,559	.883
8	Ray Allen	1,954	2,215	.882
9	Jeff Hornacek*	2,973	3,390	.877
10	Ricky Pierce*	3,389	3,871	.875

†1,200 FTM minimum

THE TOP 10
Highest 3-Pt. Field-Goal Percentages

	PLAYER	3FGM	3FGA	PCT
1	Steve Kerr*	726	1,599	.454
2	Hubert Davis	728	1,650	.441
3	Michael Redd	270	617	.438
4	Drazen Petrovic*	255	583	.437
5	Tim Legler*	260	603	.431
6	B. J. Armstrong*	436	1,026	.425
7	Steve Nash	569	1,361	.418
8	Wesley Person	1,054	2,257	.417
9	Pat Garrity	513	1,242	.413
10	Dana Barros*	1,090	2,652	.411

THREE-POINT KING

Reggie Miller of the Indiana Pacers has made the most three-pointers in NBA history. The 6-7 shooting guard has stretched out defenses with his shooting range since he entered the league in 1987, and is known as one of the greatest clutch players. The five-time NBA All-Star is the first Pacer to start in an All-Star Game.

THE TOP 10
Most Three-Point Field Goals

	PLAYER	THREE-POINTERS
1	Reggie Miller	2,330
2	Dale Ellis*	1,719
3	Glen Rice	1,554
4	Tim Hardaway	1,542
5	Dan Majerle*	1,360
6	Nick Van Exel	1,327
7	Mitch Richmond*	1,326
8	Terry Porter*	1,297
9	Mookie Blaylock*	1,283
10	Vernon Maxwell*	1,256

PHILLY'S SCORING ANSWER

He is the shortest scoring champion in NBA history yet one of the true giants of the game. Allen Iverson, the 6-0, 165-pound guard, is one of the NBA's most prolific scorers, winning three scoring titles in his first six NBA seasons. The four-time NBA All-Star is also the first player since Michael Jordan to lead the league in consecutive scoring seasons since the six-time NBA champion did it from 1995–96 to 1997–98. With his explosive quickness, fearless drives to the basket, and ability to stretch defenses with his three-point shooting, Iverson's offensive repertoire is quite expansive.

Only 10 players in NBA history have reached the 12,000-point plateau faster. Iverson surpassed this milestone in only 466 regular-season games. He boasts a single-game career high of 58 points and established a franchise single-game playoff record of 55 points during the 2003 NBA Playoffs, breaking his old mark of 54 that he had made two years earlier. Quite an impressive feat considering the Sixers' franchise has featured such greats as Wilt Chamberlain, Julius Erving, Moses Malone, and Charles Barkley.

BANK SHOT

NBA.COM FUN FACT

Joe Fulks of the Philadelphia Warriors won the first scoring title in NBA history. Jumpin' Joe averaged 23.2 points per game during the 1946–47 season.

17

THE TOP 10

Scoring Power Forwards

	PLAYER	POINTS
1	Karl Malone	36,374
2	Elvin Hayes*	27,313
3	Charles Barkley*	23,757
4	Bob Pettit*	20,880
5	Tom Chambers*	20,049
6	Terry Cummings*	19,460
7	Dolph Schayes*	19,247
8	Otis Thorpe*	17,600
9	Clifford Robinson	17,338
10	Kevin McHale*	17,335

Bob Pettit defined the power forward position in the NBA. Pettit led the St. Louis Hawks to the 1958 NBA championship, scoring a then-record 50 points in the Game 6 clincher of the 1958 NBA Finals versus the Boston Celtics.

KING CHARLES

Only four players in NBA history have accumulated 20,000 points, 10,000 rebounds, and 4,000 assists and Charles Barkley is one of them. At 6-6, he dominated the competition and opponents much taller than him.

RARIFIED AIR

Michael Jordan elevated above his competition by netting an NBA-record 10 scoring titles, which included seven in a row. In only his third season, Jordan averaged 37.1 points per game, which turned out to be his career high. Jordan also owns the highest points-per-game average with 30.1.

THE TOP 10

Scoring Small Forwards

	PLAYER	POINTS
1	Dominique Wilkins*	26,668
2	John Havlicek*	26,395
3	Alex English*	25,613
4	Adrian Dantley*	23,177
5	Elgin Baylor*	23,149
6	Larry Bird*	21,791
7	George Gervin*	20,708
8	Bernard King*	19,655
9	Walter Davis*	19,521
10	Eddie A. Johnson*	19,202

Dominique "The Human Highlight Film" Wilkins was one of the more spectacular NBA players with his 360-degree reverse windmill jams and behind-the-back reverse dunks.

THE TOP 10

Scoring Centers

	PLAYER	POINTS
1	Kareem Abdul-Jabbar*	38,387
2	Wilt Chamberlain*	31,419
3	Moses Malone*	27,409
4	Hakeem Olajuwon*	26,946
5	Patrick Ewing*	24,815
6	Robert Parish*	23,334
7	Walt Bellamy*	20,941
8	David Robinson*	20,790
9	Shaquille O'Neal	20,475
10	Bob Lanier*	19,248

Often overshadowed by his higher profile teammates Larry Bird and Kevin McHale, Robert Parish of the Boston Celtics emerged as one of the greatest centers of all time.

WILT'S 100-POINT GAME

The legend of Wilt Chamberlain was officially born on March 2, 1962, in Hershey, Pennsylvania, when only 4,124 fans witnessed the unthinkable: one man scoring 100 points in a single game. No player in NBA history has ever come close to that mark, including Chamberlain himself, who also owns the second-highest single-game scoring mark with 78 points.

Nicknamed "The Big Dipper," Chamberlain scored 41 points in the first half and followed up with 28 more in the third quarter, for a total of 69. Sensing what was at stake, fans began chanting Chamberlain's name throughout the fourth quarter, encouraging him to reach the 100-point milestone. When Wilt did hit the century mark with less than 50 seconds remaining, there was some debate as to whether the final basket was a layup or a dunk. But what isn't disputed was the accomplishment: Chamberlain scored 100 points—in one game.

THE TOP 10
Scoring Shooting Guards

	PLAYER	POINTS
1	Michael Jordan*	32,292
2	Oscar Robertson*	26,710
3	Jerry West*	25,192
4	Reggie Miller	23,505
5	Clyde Drexler*	22,195
6	Hal Greer*	21,586
7	Mitch Richmond*	20,497
8	Reggie Theus*	19,015
9	Dale Ellis*	19,004
10	Dave Bing*	18,327

The brilliance of Oscar Robertson didn't lie merely with points. He averaged a triple-double—double figures in points, rebounds, and assists—during his second season in the NBA.

THE TOP 10
Scoring Point Guards

	PLAYER	POINTS
1	John Stockton*	19,711
2	Gail Goodrich*	19,181
3	Isiah Thomas*	18,822
4	Gary Payton	18,757
5	Calvin Murphy*	17,949
6	Lenny Wilkens*	17,772
7	Magic Johnson*	17,707
8	Bob Cousy*	16,960
9	Nate Archibald*	16,481
10	Derek Harper*	16,006

The NBA's all-time leader in steals and assists, John Stockton's scoring ability was often overlooked. Yet he shot an impressive .515 percent from the field for his career.

CHAMPIONSHIP DRIVE
Isiah Thomas brought leadership, a winning attitude, and tremendous all-around skills to the Detroit Pistons franchise, leading the Pistons to back-to-back titles and netting NBA Finals MVP honors in 1990.

RUSSELL VS. CHAMBERLAIN

The greatest individual rivalry in NBA history was between Bill Russell and Wilt Chamberlain, who met 142 times throughout their Hall-of-Fame careers. Chamberlain was the ultimate offensive scoring machine while Russell was considered a revolutionary defensive force.

THE TOP 10

Most Points

	PLAYER/TEAM		DATE	FG	FT	PTS
1	**Wilt Chamberlain***	PHI	03/02/62	36	28	100
2	**Wilt Chamberlain***	PHI	12/08/61	31	16	78
3=	**Wilt Chamberlain***	PHI	01/13/62	29	15	73
=	**Wilt Chamberlain***	PHI	11/16/62	29	15	73
=	**David Thompson***	DEN	04/09/78	28	17	73
6	**Wilt Chamberlain***	PHI	11/03/62	29	14	72
7=	**Elgin Baylor***	LAL	11/15/60	28	15	71
=	**David Robinson***	SAN	04/24/94	26	18	71
9	**Wilt Chamberlain***	SF	03/10/63	27	16	70
10	**Michael Jordan***	CHI	03/28/90	23	21	69

Wilt Chamberlain's 100-point game, achieved while he was a member of the Philadelphia Warriors as they defeated the New York Knicks, 169-147, has remained an unbelievable single-game record.

THE TOP 10

Most Free Throws

	PLAYER/TEAM		DATE	FTM	FTA
1=	**Wilt Chamberlain***	PHI	03/02/62	28	32
=	**Adrian Dantley***	UT	01/04/84	28	29
3	**Adrian Dantley***	UT	11/25/83	27	31
4=	**Adrian Dantley***	UT	10/31/80	26	29
=	**Michael Jordan***	CHI	02/26/87	26	27
6=	**Frank Selvy***	MIL	12/02/54	24	26
=	**Willie Burton***	PHI	12/13/94	24	28
8=	**Dolph Schayes***	SYR	01/17/52	23	27
=	**Nate Archibald***	CIN	02/05/72	23	24
=	**Nate Archibald***	KC	01/21/75	23	25
=	**Pete Maravich***	NO	10/26/75	23	26
=	**Kevin Johnson***	PHO	04/09/90	23	24
=	**Dominique Wilkins***	ATL	12/08/92	23	23
=	**Kobe Bryant**	LAL	01/30/00	23	26

Although Wilt Chamberlain averaged only .511 percent from the free-throw line for his career, he was in the zone on the night of March 2, 1962. Twenty-eight of Chamberlain's record 100 points came from the free-throw line. "The Big Dipper" only missed four free-throw attempts on that historic night, finishing 28 of 32.

THE TOP 10

Most Field Goals

	PLAYER/TEAM		DATE	FG	FGA
1	Wilt Chamberlain*	PHI	03/02/62	36	63
2	Wilt Chamberlain*	PHI	12/08/61	31	62
3=	Wilt Chamberlain*	PHI	12/16/67	30	40
=	Rick Barry*	GS	03/26/74	30	45
5=	Wilt Chamberlain*	PHI	01/13/62	29	48
=	Wilt Chamberlain*	PHI	11/03/62	29	48
=	Wilt Chamberlain*	PHI	11/16/62	29	43
=	Wilt Chamberlain*	PHI	02/09/69	29	35
9=	Elgin Baylor*	LAL	11/15/60	28	48
=	Wilt Chamberlain*	PHI	12/09/61	28	48
=	Wilt Chamberlain*	SF	01/11/63	28	47
=	Wilt Chamberlain*	PHI	02/07/66	28	43
=	David Thompson*	DEN	04/09/78	28	38

THE TOP 10

Most Rebounds

	PLAYER/TEAM		DATE	REBOUNDS
1	Wilt Chamberlain*	PHI	11/24/60	55
2	Bill Russell*	BOS	02/05/60	51
3=	Bill Russell*	BOS	11/16/57	49
=	Bill Russell*	BOS	03/11/65	49
5=	Wilt Chamberlain*	PHI	02/06/60	45
=	Wilt Chamberlain*	PHI	01/21/61	45
7=	Wilt Chamberlain*	PHI	11/10/59	43
=	Wilt Chamberlain*	PHI	12/08/61	43
=	Bill Russell*	BOS	01/20/63	43
=	Wilt Chamberlain*	PHI	03/06/65	43

THE TOP 10

Most Steals

	PLAYER/TEAM		DATE	STEALS
1=	Larry Kenon*	SAN	12/26/76	11
=	Kendall Gill	NJ	04/03/99	11
2	Many tied with			10

THE TOP 10

Most Assists

	PLAYER/TEAM		DATE	ASSISTS
1	Scott Skiles*	ORL	12/30/90	30
2	Kevin Porter*	NJ	02/24/78	29
3=	Bob Cousy*	BOS	02/27/59	28
=	Guy Rodgers*	SF	03/14/63	28
=	John Stockton*	UT	01/15/91	28
6=	Geoff Huston*	CLE	01/27/82	27
=	John Stockton*	UT	12/19/89	27
8	John Stockton*	UT	04/14/88	26
9=	Ernie DiGregorio*	BUF	01/01/74	25
=	Kevin Porter*	DET	03/09/79	25
=	Kevin Porter*	DET	04/01/79	25
=	Isiah Thomas*	DET	02/13/85	25
=	Nate McMillan*	SEA	02/23/87	25
=	Kevin Johnson*	PHO	04/06/97	25
=	Jason Kidd	DAL	02/08/96	25

DEFENSIVE FORCE

How dominant of a shot blocker was Mark Eaton? The 7-4 center played 10 years in the NBA and posted the highest blocks-per-game average in four of those seasons. Eaton earned two NBA Defensive Player of the Year honors as well.

THE TOP 10

Most Blocked Shots

	PLAYER/TEAM		DATE	BLOCKS
1	Elmore Smith*	LAL	10/28/73	17
2=	Manute Bol*	WAS	01/25/86	15
=	Manute Bol*	WAS	02/26/87	15
=	Shaquille O'Neal	ORL	11/20/93	15
5=	Elmore Smith*	LAL	10/26/73	14
=	Elmore Smith*	LAL	11/04/73	14
=	Mark Eaton*	UT	01/18/85	14
=	Mark Eaton*	UT	02/18/89	14
9=	George Johnson*	SAN	02/24/81	13
=	Mark Eaton*	UT	02/18/83	13
=	Darryl Dawkins*	NJ	11/05/83	13
=	Ralph Sampson*	HOU	12/09/83	13
=	Manute Bol*	GS	02/02/90	13
=	Shawn Bradley	DAL	04/07/98	13

DISHING THE ROCK

Scott Skiles of the Orlando Magic entered the NBA record books when he dished 30 assists versus the Denver Nuggets on December 30, 1990. The 6-1 guard thrilled the sellout crowd of 15,077 as the Magic routed the Nuggets, 155-116.

NBA.COM FUN FACT

Scott Skiles broke the single-game assist record with only 19.6 seconds left in regulation. Skiles was stuck on 29 assists when he dished to teammate Jerry Reynolds, who hit a 22-footer.

21

ROCKET LAUNCHER

Calvin Murphy enjoyed a 13-year All-Star career with the Houston Rockets, and he was one of only two players in NBA history to shoot over 90 percent from the free-throw line for five straight seasons. His No. 23 is retired by the Rockets.

THE TOP 10

Highest Free-Throw Percentages

	PLAYER	PCT	SEASON
1	Calvin Murphy*	.958	1980–81
2	Mahmoud Abdul-Rauf*	.956	1993–94
3	Jeff Hornacek*	.950	1999–00
4	Mark Price*	.948	1992–93
5	=Mark Price*	.947	1991–92
	=Rick Barry*	.947	1978–79
7	Ernie DiGregorio*	.945	1976–77
8	Chris Mullin*	.939	1997–98
9	Rick Barry*	.935	1979–80
10	Spud Webb*	.934	1994–95

THE TOP 10

Leading Scorers

	PLAYER	PTS	SEASON
1	Wilt Chamberlain*	50.4	1961–62
2	Wilt Chamberlain*	44.8	1962–63
3	Wilt Chamberlain*	38.4	1960–61
4	Wilt Chamberlain*	37.6	1959–60
5	Michael Jordan*	37.1	1986–87
6	Wilt Chamberlain*	36.9	1963–64
7	Rick Barry*	35.6	1966–67
8	Michael Jordan*	35.0	1987–88
9	Kareem Abdul-Jabbar*	34.8	1971–72
10	Wilt Chamberlain*	34.7	1964–65

Many consider it the greatest individual season in NBA history and, after one look at the statistics, it's difficult to argue. Wilt Chamberlain not only averaged a blistering 50.4 points per game during the 1961–62 season, but he also led the league in rebounds and minutes, and scored his 100-point game. Wilt did all of this in only his third season.

THE TOP 10

Highest Field-Goal Percentages

	PLAYER	PCT	SEASON
1	Wilt Chamberlain*	.727	1972–73
2	Wilt Chamberlain*	.683	1966–67
3	Artis Gilmore*	.670	1980–81
4	Artis Gilmore*	.652	1981–82
5	Wilt Chamberlain*	.649	1971–72
6	James Donaldson*	.637	1984–85
7	Chris Gatling*	.633	1994–95
8	Steve Johnson*	.632	1985–86
9	Artis Gilmore*	.631	1983–84
10	Artis Gilmore*	.626	1982–83

THE A-TRAIN

Artis "The A-Train" Gilmore enjoyed a 12-year NBA career, five of which were spent with the San Antonio Spurs. At 7-2, Gilmore made the most of his shot opportunities. He owns the record for highest field-goal percentage with a .599 mark.

DID YOU KNOW?
Calvin Murphy's 17,949 career points ranks only second behind Hakeem Olajuwon in the Houston Rockets' record books. His 4,402 assists still rank as a Rockets' franchise record.

THE TOP 10

Highest Three-Point Field-Goal Percentages

	PLAYER	PCT	SEASON
1	Steve Kerr*	.524	1994–95
2=	Tim Legler*	.522	1995–96
=	Jon Sundvold*	.522	1988–89
4	Steve Kerr*	.507	1989–90
5=	Hubert Davis*	.491	1999–00
=	Craig Hodges*	.491	1987–88
7	Kiki Vandeweghe*	.481	1986–87
8=	Brent Barry	.476	2000–01
=	Dell Curry*	.476	1998–99
10	Steve Smith	.472	2001–02

He was the 50th overall selection in the 1988 NBA Draft yet managed to defy the odds and enjoy a 15-year NBA career. How? Steve Kerr was an excellent three-point shooter. The 6-3 guard shot an impressive .524 percent as a member of the Chicago Bulls in the 1994–95 season.

THE TOP 10

Most Rebounds

	PLAYER	REBOUNDS	SEASON
1	Wilt Chamberlain*	27.2	1960–61
2	Wilt Chamberlain*	27.0	1959–60
3	Wilt Chamberlain*	25.7	1961–62
4	Bill Russell*	24.7	1963–64
5	Wilt Chamberlain*	24.6	1965–66
6	Wilt Chamberlain*	24.3	1962–63
7	Wilt Chamberlain*	24.2	1966–67
8	Bill Russell*	24.1	1964–65
9	Wilt Chamberlain*	23.8	1967–68
10	Bill Russell*	23.0	1958–59

The greatness of Wilt Chamberlain and Bill Russell is further evidenced by one glance at the all-time single-season rebounding leaders' chart. No other player in NBA history has been able to crack the Top 10. Chamberlain's 27.0 average, which ranks second on the all-time list, was established in his rookie season.

THE TOP 10

Most Assists

	PLAYER	ASSISTS	SEASON
1	John Stockton*	14.5	1989–90
2	John Stockton*	14.2	1990–91
3	Isiah Thomas*	13.9	1984–85
4	John Stockton*	13.8	1987–88
5	John Stockton*	13.7	1991–92
6	John Stockton*	13.6	1988–89
7	Kevin Porter*	13.4	1978–79
8	Magic Johnson*	13.1	1983–84
9=	John Stockton*	12.6	1993–94
=	Magic Johnson*	12.6	1985–86

LOW-KEY SUPERSTAR

John Stockton avoided the spotlight, preferring to let his game do the talking—and it usually spoke volumes. Stockton is listed six times in the Top 10 single-season assists chart and his all-time record of 15,806 assists may never be broken.

THE TOP 10

Most Steals

	PLAYER	STEALS	SEASON
1	Alvin Robertson*	3.67	1985–86
2	Don Buse*	3.47	1976–77
3	Magic Johnson*	3.43	1980–81
4	Micheal Ray Richardson*	3.23	1979–80
5=	John Stockton*	3.21	1988–89
=	Alvin Robertson*	3.21	1986–87
7	Don Watts*	3.18	1975–76
8	Michael Jordan*	3.16	1987–88
9	Alvin Robertson*	3.04	1990–91
10	John Stockton*	2.98	1991–92

In order to be successful in the art of the theft, you must possess quick hands and the ability to anticipate. So it's not surprising to find the list of Top 10 leaders for single-season steals to be comprised of all guards. Alvin Robertson, a former 10-year veteran guard, is listed twice as a Spur and once as a Buck.

THE TOP 10

Most Minutes Played

	PLAYER	MINUTES	SEASON
1	Wilt Chamberlain*	3,882	1961–62
2	Wilt Chamberlain*	3,836	1967–68
3	Wilt Chamberlain*	3,806	1962–63
4	Wilt Chamberlain*	3,773	1960–61
5	Wilt Chamberlain*	3,737	1965–66
6	John Havlicek*	3,698	1971–72
7	Elvin Hayes*	3,695	1968–69
8	Wilt Chamberlain*	3,689	1963–64
9	Wilt Chamberlain*	3,682	1966–67
10	Nate Archibald*	3,681	1972–73

There are 48 minutes in an NBA game yet Wilt Chamberlain managed to average 48.5 during the 1961–62 season. How? The Philadelphia Warriors ended up playing seven overtime games that season (one triple, one double, and five single). According to Harvey Pollack, the Sixers' statistical guru, Chamberlain only missed eight minutes that entire season due to an ejection.

All-Time Overall Records

	TEAM	W	L	PCT
1	Los Angeles Lakers	2,671	1,648	.618
2	Chicago Stags*	145	92	.612
3	Boston Celtics	2,656	1,773	.600
4	Washington Capitols*	157	114	.579
5	Anderson Packers*	37	27	.578
6	San Antonio Spurs	1,256	926	.576
7	Portland Trail Blazers	1,467	1,207	.549
8	Phoenix Suns	1,533	1,285	.547
9	Utah Jazz	1,279	1,067	.545
10	Milwaukee Bucks	1,545	1,293	.544

SETTING THE STANDARD

Red Auerbach was the architect and coach of the greatest dynasty in NBA history, the Boston Celtics. He compiled 938 victories, then an NBA record, and guided the Celtics to nine championships.

BLAZERMANIA TAKES OVER

When the Portland Trail Blazers drafted Bill Walton as the No. 1 overall pick in the 1974 NBA Draft, hope abounded. After all, the Blazers joined the NBA in 1970, and suffered four losing seasons. But now they had acquired the three-time College Player of the Year who led the UCLA Bruins to two NCAA titles. After two injury-filled seasons, everything came together in Walton's third NBA season. The 6-11 center dominated the competition, averaging 18.6 points per game while leading the league in rebounding (14.4) and blocked shots (3.25).

The Blazers marched through the playoffs, defeating the Denver Nuggets and Los Angeles Lakers. Portland was down 0-2 to the heavily favored Philadelphia 76ers in the NBA Finals but managed to win four straight for the 1977 NBA title. Walton (center) and his teammates Maurice Lucas, Lionel Hollins, Bobby Gross, along with the superb coaching of Jack Ramsay, fueled Blazermania in Portland.

All-Time Home Records

	TEAM	W	L	PCT
1	Los Angeles Lakers	1,513	514	.746
2	Washington Capitols*	98	37	.726
3	Anderson Packers*	23	9	.719
4	Boston Celtics	1,452	574	.717
5	San Antonio Spurs	774	317	.709
6	Phoenix Suns	989	422	.701
7	Utah Jazz	821	352	.700
8=	Indianapolis Olympians*	86	37	.699
=	Portland Trail Blazers	932	402	.699
10	Chicago Stags*	70	33	.680

The Lakers called Minneapolis home for 12 seasons before moving west to sunny Los Angeles. The Minneapolis Lakers established themselves as the first dynasty in NBA history, winning five championships in six seasons. The Lakers have won nine championships since the team moved to L.A. in 1960. The combined 14 NBA titles are second only to the Boston Celtics.

DR. JAY

Julius Erving starred for 11 seasons for the Philadelphia 76ers and led them to four NBA Finals appearances in seven years. The 6-7 superstar forward averaged 22 points and 6.7 rebounds for his career, which included one NBA MVP award and 11 NBA All-Star appearances.

THE TOP 10
All-Time Road Records

	TEAM	W	L	PCT
1	Chicago Stags*	63	58	.521
2	Los Angeles Lakers	1,018	1,012	.501
3	Boston Celtics	1,002	1,111	.474
4	=Washington Capitols*	57	72	.442
	=San Antonio Spurs	482	609	.442
6	Cleveland Rebels*	13	17	.433
7	Milwaukee Bucks	595	811	.423
8	Philadelphia 76ers	829	1,162	.416
9	Portland Trail Blazers	533	793	.402
10	Seattle SuperSonics	577	859	.402

The Lakers have long been a top road draw in NBA history. Some of the league's greatest players—George Mikan, Elgin Baylor, Jerry West, Wilt Chamberlain, Kareem Abdul-Jabbar, and Magic Johnson—have starred for this franchise.

THE TOP 10
Neutral Court Records†

	TEAM	W	L	PCT
1	Anderson Duffey Packers*	3	0	1.000
2	Chicago Stags*	12	1	.923
3	Boston Celtics	202	88	.697
4	Milwaukee Bucks	24	15	.615
5	Indianapolis Olympians*	15	11	.577
6	St. Louis Bombers*	4	3	.571
7	Golden State Warriors††	165	130	.559
8	Philadelphia 76ers	161	133	.548
9	Cleveland Cavaliers	6	5	.545
10	Los Angeles Lakers	140	122	.534

† Neutral-court records kept before 1973–74 season.
†† Club located in San Francisco

All-Time Winningest Coaches†

	COACH	W	L	PCT
1	Lenny Wilkens	1,292	1,114	.537
2	Pat Riley	1,110	569	.661
3	Don Nelson	1,096	828	.570
4	Bill Fitch*	944	1,106	.460
5	Red Auerbach*	938	479	.662
6	Dick Motta*	935	1,017	.479
7	Larry Brown	879	685	.627
8	Jerry Sloan	875	521	.627
9	Jack Ramsay*	864	783	.525
10	Cotton Fitzsimmons*	832	775	.518

† Coaches who have won 200+ games

All-Time Coaches Ranked by Games

	COACH	GAMES
1	Lenny Wilkens	2,406
2	Bill Fitch*	2,050
3	Dick Motta*	1,952
4	Don Nelson	1,924
5	Pat Riley	1,679
6	Jack Ramsay*	1,647
7	Gene Shue*	1,645
8	Cotton Fitzsimmons*	1,607
9	Larry Brown	1,564
10	Red Auerbach*	1,417

THE COACHING LEADER

Lenny Wilkens owns the distinction of being one of only two men to be inducted into the Naismith Memorial Basketball Hall of Fame as a player and as a coach. Wilkens is the NBA's all-time leader in victories with 1,292 wins.

All-Time Coaches Ranked by Winning Percentage†

	COACH	PCT	W	L
1	Phil Jackson	.728	776	290
2	Billy Cunningham*	.698	454	196
3	K. C. Jones*	.674	522	252
4	Red Auerbach*	.662	938	479
5	Pat Riley	.661	1,110	569
6	Gregg Popovich	.647	339	185
7=	Jerry Sloan	.627	875	521
=	Paul Westphal*	.627	267	159
9	Lester Harrison*	.620	95	181
10	Tom Heinsohn*	.619	427	263

† 400 games minimum

FROM PLAYER TO COACH

Playing as a New York Knick, Phil Jackson learned from one of the game's best coaches, Red Holzman. Jackson did his mentor proud, coaching the Chicago Bulls to six NBA titles and three with the L.A. Lakers.

THE LEGEND OF RED

Red Auerbach's coaching career began with the Washington Capitols of the Basketball Association of America, where he proved early on that he had the winning touch, leading them to two division titles (1947 and 1949). After one season with the Tri-Cities BlackHawks, Auerbach (left) was named VP and head coach of the Boston Celtics. After several successful seasons leading Boston to the playoffs, Auerbach changed the Celtics' fortunes for good in April of 1956, when he acquired three future Hall of Famers—K. C. Jones, Tom Heinsohn, and Bill Russell (pictured)—laying the foundation for the greatest dynasty in NBA history.

The Celtics proceeded to win nine championships over the course of the next 10 years, including a record eight in a row. The fiery Auerbach led the Celtics to 10 Eastern Division titles in 16 years and 99 playoff victories. As a result of his success, Auerbach coached 11 NBA All-Star Games and was named NBA Coach of the Year in 1965. Auerbach retired from coaching in 1968, but remained the team's general manager, maintaining a major role in the franchise's seven additional NBA championships.

BANK SHOT

STREAKS

THE LAKERS MAKE NBA HISTORY

The 1971–72 season was significant for the Los Angeles Lakers in more ways than one. The Lakers made NBA history when they posted the greatest single-season record with a 69-13 mark, which included a record 33 consecutive wins. Los Angeles also ended their NBA Finals drought. The Lakers were 0-7 in Finals competition since the team moved from Minneapolis to Los Angeles in 1960. The '71–72 team saw that streak come to an end by defeating the New York Knicks in the 1972 Finals.

THE TOP 10
Overall Winning Percentages

	TEAM	SEASON	RECORD	PCT
1	Chicago	1995–96	(72-10)	.878
2=	L.A. Lakers	1971–72	(69-13)	.841
=	Chicago	1996–97	(69-13)	.841
4	Philadelphia	1966–67	(68-13)	.840
5	Boston	1972–73	(69-14)	.829
6=	Boston	1985–86	(67-15)	.817
=	Chicago	1991–92	(67-15)	.817
=	L.A. Lakers	1999–00	(67-15)	.817
9	Washington	1946–47	(49-11)	.816
10	Milwaukee	1970–71	(66-16)	.805

THE TOP 10
Home Winning Percentages

	TEAM	SEASON	RECORD	PCT
1	Boston	1985–86	(40-1)	.976
2	Rochester*	1949–50	(33-1)	.971
3	Syracuse*	1949–50	(31-1)	.969
4	Minneapolis*	1949–50	(30-1)	.968
5	Washington	1946–47	(29-1)	.967
6=	Boston	1986–87	(39-2)	.951
=	Orlando	1994–95	(39-2)	.951
=	Chicago	1995–96	(39-2)	.951
=	Chicago	1996–97	(39-2)	.951
10	Milwaukee	1970–71	(34-2)	.944

In 1996, the 1985–86 Boston Celtics were voted as one of the Top 10 Teams in NBA History, featuring Hall of Famers such as Larry Bird, Kevin McHale, Robert Parish, and Bill Walton. The Celtics cruised to a 40-1 home record, en route to a 67-15 overall mark, and the franchise's 16th championship title. The Celtics defeated the Houston Rockets in six games.

THE TOP 10
Road Winning Percentages

	TEAM	SEASON	RECORD	PCT
1	L.A. Lakers	1971–72	(31-7)	.816
2	Chicago	1995–96	(33-8)	.805
3	Boston	1972–73	(32-8)	.800
4=	Boston	1974–75	(32-9)	.780
=	Miami	1996–97	(32-9)	.780
6	Philadelphia	1966–67	(26-8)	.765
7=	Chicago	1991–92	(31-10)	.756
=	L.A. Lakers	1999–00	(31-10)	.756
9=	Philadelphia	1982–83	(30-11)	.732
=	Chicago	1996–97	(30-11)	.732

TEAM FOR THE AGES

The 1995–96 Chicago Bulls made NBA history when they became the first team to win 70 or more games in a season. The Bulls went 72-10, which included a 33-8 record on the road. However, the regular-season mark wouldn't have carried nearly as much weight had Chicago not won the NBA title that season.

Most Consecutive 35-Plus-Point Games (by Michael Jordan)

	POINTS	GAME	DATE
1	37	at Denver	11/26/86
2	41	at Los Angeles	11/28/86
3	40	at Golden State	1/29/86
4	40	at Seattle	12/2/86
5	45	at Utah	12/3/86
6	43	at Phoenix	12/5/86
7	43	at San Antonio	12/6/86
8	40	at Denver	12/9/86
9	41	at Atlanta	12/10/86
10	41	at Milwaukee	12/12/86

Michael Jordan was on a roll during the 1986–87 season when he scored 35 or more points for 10 consecutive games. However, Wilt Chamberlain owns the top three records for such a streak with 33, 23, and 20 games, respectively. Kobe Bryant moved into fourth place behind Chamberlain with 13 when he accomplished this during the 2002–03 season.

THE NBA'S IRON MAN

No one has played in more consecutive games than A. C. Green. The 6-9 forward played in 1,192 consecutive contests, breaking the previous mark of 907 held by Randy Smith. Green was a member of the Dallas Mavericks when he became the NBA's new iron man, a record he set on November 21, 1997. A special 23-minute half-time celebration was held for Green, which featured videotaped tributes from former Los Angeles Laker teammates Magic Johnson and James Worthy, and included Smith and Cal Ripken, Jr.—Major League Baseball's iron man, who is quoted below—in attendance.

"I know that in the 10 or 11 years during which this streak has existed, there had to be many nights where his body said, 'No,' but somewhere down deep inside, he had to go down there and dig it out and say, 'I'm going to do it, I'm going to go out and play.' That's spirit; that's heart."

The 23rd overall selection in the 1985 NBA Draft, Green enjoyed a 15-year career and was a member of three Los Angeles Laker NBA championship teams.

Winning Streaks

	TEAM	GAMES	DATE
1	L.A. Lakers	33	11/5/71–1/7/72
2=	Milwaukee	20	2/6/71–3/8/71
=	Boston	20	2/24/82–3/26/82
4=	Chicago	18	12/29/95–2/2/96
=	New York	18	10/24/69–11/28/69
6	San Antonio	17	2/29/96–3/31/96
7	Portland	16	3/20/91–4/19/91
8=	Houston	15	2/13/93–3/18/93
=	Sacramento*†	15	2/17/50–3/19/50
=	Utah	15	11/13/96–12/10/96

† Club located in Rochester

The most impressive team winning streak in NBA history occurred when the 1971–72 Los Angeles Lakers won 33—in a row. The streak began on November 5, 1971, against the Baltimore Bullets, and lasted until January 7, 1972, with a defeat of the Atlanta Hawks. The Lakers saw their streak end in Milwaukee to the Bucks, 120-104.

Losing Streaks

	TEAM	GAMES	DATE
1=	Denver	23	12/9/97–1/23/98
=	Memphis†	23	2/16/96–4/2/96
3=	Dallas	20	11/13/93–12/22/93
=	Philadelphia	20	1/9/73–2/11/73
5=	Cleveland	19	3/19/82–4/18/82
=	L.A. Clippers††	19	3/11/82–4/13/82
=	L.A. Clippers	19	12/30/88–2/6/89
8	Utah	18	2/24/82–3/29/82
9=	Golden State	17	12/20/64–1/26/65
=	Houston	17	1/18/68–2/16/68
=	Miami	17	11/5/88–12/12/88
=	Orlando	17	12/4/91–1/7/92
=	Toronto	17	11/6/97–12/9/97

† Club located in Vancouver

†† Club located in San Diego

THE TOP 10

Most Rebounds
Total

	PLAYER	REBOUNDS
1	Wilt Chamberlain*	23,924
2	Bill Russell*	21,620
3	Kareem Abdul-Jabbar*	17,440
4	Elvin Hayes*	16,279
5	Moses Malone*	16,212
6	Robert Parish*	14,715
7	Karl Malone	14,601
8	Nate Thurmond*	14,464
9	Walt Bellamy*	14,241
10	Wes Unseld*	13,769

Often overshadowed by his scoring brilliance was Wilt Chamberlain's tremendous ability to rebound the ball. The 13-time NBA All-Star averaged 22.9 rebounds per game over his 14-year career. In only his second season, "The Big Dipper" set the NBA single-season record with 2,149 rebounds, for a 27.2 per-game average. He led the league in rebounding in all but three of his seasons playing. Chamberlain was elected to the Naismith Memorial Basketball Hall of Fame in 1978.

THE TOP 10

Most Steals

	PLAYER	STEALS
1	John Stockton*	3,265
2	Michael Jordan*	2,514
3	Maurice Cheeks*	2,310
4	Scottie Pippen	2,286
5	Clyde Drexler*	2,207
6	Hakeem Olajuwon*	2,162
7	Gary Payton	2,147
8	Alvin Robertson*	2,112
9	Mookie Blaylock*	2,075
10	Karl Malone	2,035

Few knew what to expect from John Stockton, the 16th overall pick who wasn't exactly a household name coming out of Gonzaga University in 1984. But Stockton's brilliant career includes numerous records, such as the all-time leader in steals.

DEFENSIVE STAR

Mark Eaton played his entire 10-year career in Salt Lake City and was a valuable member of the Jazz. Eaton was a shot-blocking machine, routinely rejecting opponents' shot attempts. In 1984–85, he set a single-season record of 5.56 blocks per game.

THE TOP 10

Most Blocked
Shots

	PLAYER	BLOCKS
1	Hakeem Olajuwon*	3,830
2	Kareem Abdul-Jabbar*	3,189
3	Mark Eaton*	3,064
4	David Robinson*	2,954
5	Patrick Ewing*	2,894
6	Dikembe Mutombo	2,873
7	Tree Rollins*	2,542
8	Robert Parish*	2,361
9	Manute Bol*	2,086
10	George T. Johnson*	2,082

THE TOP 10

Most Defensive
Rebounds

	PLAYER	DEFENSIVE REBOUNDS
1	Karl Malone	11,100
2	Robert Parish*	10,117
3	Hakeem Olajuwon*	9,714
4	Moses Malone*	9,481
5	Kareem Abdul-Jabbar*	9,394
6	Patrick Ewing*	8,855
7	Buck Williams*	8,491
8	Charles Barkley*	8,286
9	Charles Oakley	8,276
10	Jack Sikma*	8,274

Jack Sikma spent the first nine years of his 14-year career with the Seattle SuperSonics and was selected to the NBA's All-Star Game seven times. Sikma helped the Sonics win the 1979 NBA Finals title and is the team's all-time leading rebounder.

THE TOP 10

Rebounding Title
Winners

	PLAYER	REBOUNDING TITLES
1	Wilt Chamberlain*	11
2	Dennis Rodman*	7
3	Moses Malone*	6
4	Bill Russell*	4
5 =	Elvin Hayes*	2
=	Dikembe Mutombo	2
=	Hakeem Olajuwon*	2
=	Ben Wallace	2
6	Many tied with	1

Moses Malone excelled at rebounding, averaging 12.2 for his 21-year Hall-of-Fame career. Making the jump to the ABA straight out of high school, Malone joined the Houston Rockets of the NBA two years later. The 6-10 center especially owned the offensive glass, leading the league in this category eight times. Malone pulled down a record 21 offensive rebounds in a single game on February 11, 1982, versus the Seattle SuperSonics.

THE TOP 10

Last NBA Defensive-Player-of-the-Year Awards

SEASON	PLAYER	TEAM
2002–03	Ben Wallace	DET
2001–02	Ben Wallace	DET
2000–01	Dikembe Mutombo	PHI
1999–00	Alonzo Mourning	MIA
1998–99	Alonzo Mourning	MIA
1997–98	Dikembe Mutombo	ATL
1996–97	Dikembe Mutombo	ATL
1995–96	Gary Payton	SEA
1994–95	Dikembe Mutombo	DEN
1993–94	Hakeem Olajuwon*	HOU

BIG BEN

At 6-9, 240 pounds, Ben Wallace is an imposing presence. Possessing a relentless work ethic, Wallace earned NBA Defensive Player of the Year and top rebounding honors in consecutive seasons.

THE TOP 10

Last Steals Leaders

SEASON	PLAYER	STEALS
2002–03	Ron Artest	2.50
2001–02	Allen Iverson	2.80
2000–01	Allen Iverson	2.51
1999–00	Eddie Jones	2.67
1998–99	Kendall Gill	2.68
1997–98	Mookie Blaylock*	2.61
1996–97	Mookie Blaylock*	2.72
1995–96	Gary Payton	2.85
1994–95	Scottie Pippen	2.94
1993–94	Nate McMillan*	2.96

Not only does Philadelphia 76er Allen Iverson excel on the offensive end, he is a whiz at defense as well. The 6-0 guard led the league in steals in consecutive seasons and also owns the single-game playoff record for most swipes. The Hampton, Virginia native recorded eight steals versus the Orlando Magic in Game 4 of the first round of the 1999 NBA Playoffs.

BILL RUSSELL: CHANGING THE GAME

No one had a greater impact on the defensive end of the game than Bill Russell. The 6-10 center revolutionized the way defense was played. Russell was the centerpiece of the greatest dynasty in NBA history, the Boston Celtics. In Russell's 13 NBA seasons, the Celtics won 11 championships, thanks in large part to the 12-time NBA All-Star's tremendous shot-blocking and rebounding abilities.

When Russell arrived in Boston in 1956, the Celtics were considered an offensive machine, featuring such future Hall of Famers as Bob Cousy and Bill Sharman. What the team lacked in defense and inside toughness, Russell more than provided. Blocked shots weren't kept as an official statistic during the years Russell played in the NBA, but if they were, there is little doubt that he would officially rank as the very best in NBA history.

The five-time NBA MVP averaged 22.5 rebounds per game for his career, led the league in rebounding four times, and proved that a player didn't have to be an offensive superstar to dominate the game. He also became the first African-American coach in the NBA, when he took over as player-coach for the Celtics for the 1966–67 season. The Monroe, Louisiana native was elected to the Naismith Memorial Basketball Hall of Fame in 1975, and was voted one of the 50 Greatest Players in NBA History in 1996.

N B A . C O M   F U N   F A C T

Ben Wallace was not drafted but signed as a free agent with the Washington Bullets on October 2, 1996, and played three seasons before being traded to Orlando and eventually landing in Detroit.

31

THE TOP 10
Most Points

	PLAYER/COUNTRY	POINTS
1	**Hakeem Olajuwon*** Nigeria	26,946
2	**Patrick Ewing*** Jamaica	24,815
3	**Rolando Blackman*** Panama	17,623
4	**Kiki Vandeweghe*** Germany	15,980
5	**Detlef Schrempf*** Germany	15,761
6	**Rik Smits*** Holland	12,871
7	**Mychal Thompson*** Bahamas	12,810
8	**Vlade Divac** Serbia-Montenegro	12,564
9	**Dikembe Mutombo** Congo (Zaire)	10,511
10	**Tim Duncan** US Virgin Islands	10,324

Born in Lagos, Nigeria, Hakeem Olajuwon excelled at soccer before turning his attention to basketball. He owns several Rockets' records, including points, rebounds, steals, and blocks.

MOUNT MUTOMBO

Dikembe Mutombo led the NBA in rebounding in back-to-back seasons (1999–00 and 2000–2001). He also holds the career record for most consecutive seasons leading the league in blocked shots per game—three (1993–94 through 1995–96).

THE TOP 10
Most Field Goals

	PLAYER/COUNTRY	FIELD GOALS
1	**Hakeem Olajuwon*** Nigeria	10,749
2	**Patrick Ewing*** Jamaica	9,702
3	**Rolando Blackman*** Panama	6,887
4	**Kiki Vandeweghe*** Germany	6,139
5	**Detlef Schrempf*** Germany	5,400
6	**Rik Smits*** Holland	5,301
7	**Mychal Thompson*** Bahamas	5,191
8	**Vlade Divac** Serbia-Montenegro	4,878
9	**Tim Duncan** US Virgin Islands	3,932
10	**Dikembe Mutombo** Congo (Zaire)	3,737

For 15 seasons, Patrick Ewing starred for the New York Knicks. The 7-0, 255-pound center from Kingston, Jamaica, owns virtually all of the franchise's major records and left the sport as the 13th all-time leading scorer with 24,814 points. In 1996, Ewing was selected as one of the 50 Greatest Players in NBA History and he earned two Olympic gold medals, one as a member of the 1992 Dream Team.

THE TOP 10
Most Free Throws

	PLAYER/COUNTRY	FREE THROWS
1	**Hakeem Olajuwon*** Nigeria	5,423
2	**Patrick Ewing*** Jamaica	5,392
3	**Detlef Schrempf*** Germany	4,486
4	**Rolando Blackman*** Panama	3,620
5	**Kiki Vandeweghe*** Germany	3,484
6	**Dikembe Mutombo** Congo (Zaire)	3,037
7	**Vlade Divac** Serbia-Montenegro	2,710
8	**Ron Seikaly*** Lebanon	2,691
9	**Tim Duncan** US Virgin Islands	2,444
10	**Mychal Thompson*** Bahamas	2,427

Rolando Blackman starred for 11 seasons with the Dallas Mavericks. The 6-6 shooting guard owns several Mavericks' records, including most points, field goals made and attempted, and free throws made and attempted. Blackman was a four-time NBA All-Star with the Mavs, and his jersey (22) has been retired by the team.

DREAM CAREER

Hakeem Olajuwon enjoyed one of the greatest careers of any big man in NBA history. The 6-10 center won numerous awards, including NBA MVP, NBA Finals MVP, and NBA Defensive Player of the Year, while also owning the career record for most blocks with 3,830.

THE TOP 10
Most Rebounds

	PLAYER/COUNTRY	REBOUNDS
1	**Hakeem Olajuwon*** Nigeria	13,748
2	**Patrick Ewing*** Jamaica	11,607
3	**Dikembe Mutombo** Congo (Zaire)	10,470
4	**Vlade Divac** Serbia-Montenegro	8,831
5	**Olden Polynice** Haiti	7,108
6	**Detlef Schrempf*** Germany	7,023
7	**Mychal Thompson*** Bahamas	6,951
8	**Thomas Meschery*** Russia	6,698
9	**Ron Seikaly*** Lebanon	6,424
10	**Tim Duncan** US Virgin Islands	5,548

Ever since he entered the NBA as a rookie in 1997, Tim Duncan of the San Antonio Spurs has never averaged less than 11.4 rebounds per season. The St. Croix native will no doubt move up on the international list of top rebounders.

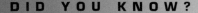

DID YOU KNOW?
Dikembe Mutombo is the Denver Nuggets' all-time blocked shots leader with 1,486 (1991–92 through 1995–96).

THE TOP 10

Most Assists

PLAYER/COUNTRY	ASSISTS
1 **Detlef Schrempf*** Germany	3,833
2 **Vlade Divac** Serbia-Montenegro	3,090
3 **Hakeem Olajuwon*** Nigeria	3,058
4 **Steve Nash** Canada	2,632
5 **Toni Kukoc** Croatia	2,620
6 **Rick Fox** Canada	2,551
7 **Patrick Ewing*** Jamaica	2,215
8 **Mychal Thompson*** Bahamas	2,141
9 **Kiki Vandeweghe*** Germany	1,668
10 **Tim Duncan** US Virgin Islands	1,447

INTERNATIONAL SUPERSTAR

Before he arrived in the NBA, Vlade Divac played for five years in his homeland of Serbia-Montenegro. In 1989, the 7-1 center joined the Los Angeles Lakers, with whom he played for five seasons, before joining the Charlotte Hornets. Divac now stars for the Sacramento Kings.

THE TOP 10

Most Steals

PLAYER/COUNTRY	STEALS
1 **Hakeem Olajuwon*** Nigeria	2,162
2 **Vlade Divac** Serbia-Montenegro	1,227
3 **Patrick Ewing*** Jamaica	1,136
4 **Rick Fox** Canada	938
5 **Detlef Schrempf*** Germany	856
6 **Rolando Blackman*** Panama	715
7 **Toni Kukoc** Croatia	686
8 **Olden Polynice** Haiti	515
9 **Ernie Grunfeld*** Romania	472
10 **Kiki Vandeweghe*** Germany	468

THE TOP 10

Most Blocked Shots

PLAYER/COUNTRY	BLOCKS
1 **Hakeem Olajuwon*** Nigeria	3,830
2 **Patrick Ewing*** Jamaica	2,894
3 **Dikembe Mutombo** Congo (Zaire)	2,873
4 **Manute Bol*** Sudan	2,086
5 **Vlade Divac** Serbia-Montenegro	1,553
6 **Tim Duncan** US Virgin Islands	1,129
7 **Rik Smits*** Holland	1,111
8 **Mychal Thompson*** Bahamas	1,073
9 **Ron Seikaly*** Lebanon	872
10 **Adonal Foyle** St. Vincent & Grenadines	760

NBA DRAFT

First No. 1 Lottery Picks

YEAR	PLAYER/COLLEGE
1985	Patrick Ewing* (Georgetown)
1986	Brad Daugherty* (North Carolina)
1987	David Robinson* (Navy)
1988	Danny Manning* (Kansas)
1989	Pervis Ellison* (Louisville)
1990	Derrick Coleman (Syracuse)
1991	Larry Johnson* (UNLV)
1992	Shaquille O'Neal (LSU)
1993	Chris Webber (Michigan)
1994	Glenn Robinson (Purdue)

The NBA Draft Lottery made its debut in 1985 to determine the order of selection for non-playoff teams or teams holding their picks through trades for the first round only. Later it was modified to give teams with the worst records a better chance at the top picks. The New York Knicks, who posted a 24-48 record, won the first lottery.

YAO-MANIA!

Yao Ming made NBA history on June 26, 2002, when the Houston Rockets selected him with the No. 1 overall pick in the NBA Draft. Yao became the first player from an international league to be selected with the top selection.

Last No. 1 Overall Draft Picks

YEAR	PLAYER/SCHOOL
2003	LeBron James (St. Vincent-St. Mary HS)
2002	Yao Ming (China)
2001	Kwame Brown (Glynn Academy HS)
2000	Kenyon Martin (Cincinnati)
1999	Elton Brand (Duke)
1998	Michael Olowokandi (Pacific)
1997	Tim Duncan (Wake Forest)
1996	Allen Iverson (Georgetown)
1995	Joe Smith (Maryland)
1994	Glenn Robinson (Purdue)

Prior to the 2003 NBA Draft, only three of the last nine overall picks have taken home NBA Rookie of the Year honors. Allen Iverson, Tim Duncan, and Elton Brand are in select company for receiving the league's highest honor for a rookie, although Brand shared his 2000 honors with Steve Francis of the Houston Rockets.

LOCAL HERO

In the early days of the NBA, teams struggled to build fan bases. A common way for teams to take advantage of local talent and build popularity was to select a college star. In doing so, the team would forfeit their first-round pick. In 1965, the New York Knicks did just that and selected Bill Bradley, the 6-5 sharp-shooting forward from Princeton University.

Bradley starred for the Princeton Tigers and scored 2,503 points during his collegiate career for a 30.2 points-per-game average. "Dollar Bill" played 10 seasons for the Knicks and was an invaluable contributor on their two championship teams (1970 and '73). The Oxford Rhodes Scholar scored more than 9,217 points for a 12.4 points-per-game average in his NBA career. Bradley was inducted in the Naismith Memorial Basketball Hall of Fame in 1982, and served as a US Senator from New Jersey for three terms, from 1979 to 1997.

BANK SHOT

First No. 1 Draft Picks

YEAR	PLAYER/COLLEGE
1957	Rod Hundley* (West Virginia)
1958	Elgin Baylor* (Seattle)
1959	Wilt Chamberlain* (Kansas)
1960	Oscar Robertson* (Cincinnati)
1961	Walt Bellamy* (Indiana)
1962	Dave DeBusschere* (Detroit)
1963	Tom Thacker* (Cincinnati)
1964	George Wilson* (Cincinnati)
1965	Bill Bradley* (Princeton)
1966	Cazzie Russell* (Michigan)

The NBA began drafting players in 1947, but early draft records are incomplete. It wasn't until the 1957 NBA Draft when it was confirmed that "Hot Rod Hundley" out of West Virginia University was the No. 1 overall pick.

ROOKIE OF THE YEAR
The winner of the 1969 NBA coin flip between the Bucks and Suns secured the opportunity to draft college basketball's most dominant player, Kareem Abdul-Jabbar. The Bucks won.

THE TOP 10

First Draft Coin Flips

YEAR	FLIP CALL	RESULT	FIRST TWO PICKS
1966	**Detroit**: Tails	Heads	New York—Cazzie Russell* Detroit—Dave Bing*
1967	**Baltimore**: Tails	Heads	Detroit—Jimmy Walker* Baltimore—Earl Malone*
1968	**San Diego**: Heads	Heads	San Diego—Elvin Hayes* Baltimore—Wes Unseld*
1969	**Phoenix**: Heads	Tails	Milwaukee— Kareem Abdul-Jabbar* Phoenix—Neal Walk*
1970	**San Diego**: Heads	Tails	Detroit—Bob Lanier* San Diego—Rudy Tomjanovich*
1971	**Portland**: Heads	Tails	Cleveland—Austin Carr* Portland—Sydney Wicks*
1972	**Portland**: Tails	Tails	Portland—LaRue Martin* Buffalo—Bob McAdoo*
1973	**Philadelphia**: Tails	Tails	Philadelphia—Doug Collins* Cleveland—Jim Brewer*
1974	**Philadelphia**: Heads	Tails	Portland—Bill Walton* Philadelphia—Marvin Barnes*
1975	**Atlanta**: Tails	Tails	Atlanta—David Thompson* L.A. Lakers—David Meyers*

THE TOP 10

Last Draft Coin Flips

YEAR	FLIP CALL	RESULT	FIRST TWO PICKS
1984	**Portland**: Tails	Heads	Houston—Hakeem Olajuwon* Portland—Sam Bowie*
1983	**Houston**: Heads	Heads	Houston—Ralph Sampson* Indiana—Steve Stipanovich*
1982	**L.A. Lakers**: Heads	Heads	L.A. Lakers—James Worthy* San Diego—Terry Cummings*
1981	**Detroit**: Heads	Tails	Dallas—Mark Aguirre* Detroit—Isiah Thomas*
1980	**Utah**: Heads	Tails	Golden State—Joe Barry Carroll* Utah—Darrell Griffith*
1979	**Chicago**: Heads	Tails	L.A. Lakers—Magic Johnson* Chicago—David Greenwood*
1978	**Kansas City**: Heads	Tails	Portland—Mychal Thompson* Kansas City—Phil Ford*
1977	**Kansas City**: Heads	Tails	Milwaukee—Kent Benson* Kansas City—Otis Birdsong*
1976	**Houston**: Heads	Heads	Houston—John Lucas* Chicago—Scott May*
1975	**Atlanta**: Tails	Tails	Atlanta—David Thompson* L.A. Lakers—David Meyers*

NBA.COM FUN FACT

Kareem Abdul-Jabbar averaged 28.8 points during his rookie season and led all NBA players with 2,361 points and field goals made with 938.

ALL-STAR PIONEERS

Boston Celtics' owner Walter Brown is flanked by "Easy" Ed Macauley (left) and Bob Cousy at the inaugural NBA All-Star Game held in Boston Garden on March 2, 1951.

THE TOP 10

Most Games Played

	PLAYER	GAMES
1	Kareem Abdul-Jabbar*	18
2=	Wilt Chamberlain*	13
=	Bob Cousy*	13
=	John Havlicek*	13
=	Michael Jordan*	13
6=	Elvin Hayes*	12
=	Karl Malone	12
=	Hakeem Olajuwon*	12
=	Oscar Robertson*	12
=	Bill Russell*	12
=	Jerry West*	12

Kareem Abdul-Jabbar was selected to the All-Star team a 19th time but could not participate.

THE TOP 10

Most Minutes Played

	PLAYER	MINUTES
1	Kareem Abdul-Jabbar*	449
2	Wilt Chamberlain*	388
3	Michael Jordan*	382
4	Oscar Robertson*	380
5	Bob Cousy*	368
6	Bob Pettit*	360
7	Bill Russell*	343
8	Jerry West*	341
9	Magic Johnson*	331
10	Elgin Baylor*	321

In 18 NBA All-Star Game appearances (six as a Milwaukee Buck and 12 as a L.A. Laker), Kareem Abdul-Jabbar averaged 24.9 minutes per contest.

THE TOP 10

Most Rebounds

	PLAYER	REBOUNDS
1	Wilt Chamberlain*	197
2	Bob Pettit*	178
3	Kareem Abdul-Jabbar*	149
4	Bill Russell*	139
5	Moses Malone*	108
6	Dolph Schayes*	105
7	Elgin Baylor*	99
8	Hakeem Olajuwon*	94
9	Elvin Hayes*	92
10	Dave Cowens*	81

DID YOU KNOW?
Bob Cousy of the Boston Celtics took home NBA All-Star Game MVP honors twice during his career. Cousy won the award in 1954 and 1957.

Most Steals

	PLAYER	STEALS
1	Michael Jordan*	37
2	Isiah Thomas*	31
3	Larry Bird*	23
4	Magic Johnson*	21
5	Gary Payton	19
6	Julius Erving*	18
7=	Jason Kidd	17
=	Scottie Pippen	17
9=	Rick Barry*	16
=	George Gervin*	16
=	John Stockton*	16

In addition to boasting one of the highest scoring averages in All-Star Game history, Michael Jordan also reigns supreme on the defensive end. In 13 appearances, he averaged 2.8 steals per game.

Most Blocked Shots

	PLAYER	BLOCKED SHOTS
1	Kareem Abdul-Jabbar*	31
2	Hakeem Olajuwon*	23
3	Patrick Ewing*	16
4	David Robinson*	13
5=	Kevin McHale*	12
=	Shaquille O'Neal	12
7	Julius Erving*	11
8	Dikembe Mutombo	10
9	George Gervin*	9
10=	Alonzo Mourning	8
=	Robert Parish*	8

George "Iceman" Gervin won four NBA scoring titles in his career and scored a personal high of 34 points in the 1980 NBA All-Star Game. The nine-time NBA All-Star also excelled in blocking.

ALL-STAR ASSISTS

A perennial NBA All-Star selection, Jason Kidd will continue to climb the all-time assists chart. The brilliant all-around point guard has made the All-Star team as a member of the Dallas Mavericks, Phoenix Suns, and New Jersey Nets.

Most Assists

	PLAYER	ASSISTS
1	Magic Johnson*	127
2	Isiah Thomas*	97
3	Bob Cousy*	86
4	Oscar Robertson*	81
5	Gary Payton	73
6	John Stockton*	71
7	Jerry West*	55
8	Michael Jordan*	54
9	Kareem Abdul-Jabbar*	51
10	Jason Kidd	48

Magic Johnson is a two-time NBA All-Star Game MVP recipient. The 12-time All-Star made 11 appearances and averaged an impressive 11.5 assists per game.

A MAGICAL AFTERNOON

The anticipation increased as each player's name was introduced at the 1992 NBA All-Star Game. After the 12 players from the East and West squads walked out onto the court, the capacity crowd of 14,272 at the Orena in Orlando, remained on their feet as the 13th All-Star for the West squad made his entrance. Magic Johnson, who retired prematurely three months earlier because he had contracted HIV, the human immunodeficiency virus that causes AIDS, briefly returned to NBA competition. First Isiah Thomas crossed the court to embrace Johnson and soon every member of the East All-Stars followed suit.

It was a triumphant return for the three-time NBA MVP, who dazzled with 25 points and nine assists to earn MVP honors in the West's 153-113 victory. Johnson put an exclamation mark on his magical performance when he lofted a three-pointer with 14.5 seconds remaining. The shot hit nothing but net as the crowd erupted and the remaining seconds ticked away as the players ran to congratulate the All-Star hero.

"It was the first game ever called on account of hugs," Johnson said.

BANK SHOT

THE TOP 10

Highest Scoring Averages†

	PLAYER	G	FGM	FTM	PTS	AVG
1	Allen Iverson	4	34	19	91	22.8
2	Kobe Bryant	5	43	12	105	21.0
3	Oscar Robertson*	12	88	70	246	20.5
4	Bob Pettit*	11	81	62	224	20.4
5	Michael Jordan*	13	110	39	262	20.2
6	Julius Erving*	11	85	50	221	20.1
7	Elgin Baylor*	11	70	78	218	19.8
8	George Mikan*	4	28	22	78	19.5
9	Paul Westphal*	5	43	11	97	19.4
10	Tom Chambers*	4	29	17	77	19.3

† 3 games or 60 points minimum

ALL-STAR PERFORMER

Allen Iverson holds the highest scoring average in All-Star Game history and took home MVP honors of the 2001 classic in Washington, D.C. Iverson scored 15 of his 25 points in the final nine minutes of regulation in the East's 111-110 comeback victory.

STAR OF STARS

Michael Jordan owns three All-Star Game MVPs and recorded the only triple-double in NBA All-Star Game history. Jordan scored 14 points, grabbed 11 rebounds, and dished 11 assists in the East's 132-120 victory over the West in Cleveland in 1997.

THE TOP 10

Most Points

	PLAYER	POINTS
1	Michael Jordan*	262
2	Kareem Abdul-Jabbar*	251
3	Oscar Robertson*	246
4	Bob Pettit*	224
5	Julius Erving*	221
6	Elgin Baylor*	218
7	Wilt Chamberlain*	191
8	Isiah Thomas*	185
9	John Havlicek*	179
10	Magic Johnson*	176

In 13 NBA All-Star appearances, Michael Jordan scored a total of 262 points for a 20.1 scoring average. The 10-time NBA scoring champion scored a personal single–All-Star Game high of 40 points in the 1987 classic in Seattle.

The Top 10 Most Free Throws

Player/Free Throws

1 Elgin Baylor* 78 **2** Oscar Robertson* 70 **3** Bob Pettit* 62 **4** Julius Erving* 50
5 Wilt Chamberlain* 47 **6** Bob Cousy* 43 **7** Dolph Schayes* 42 **8** = Kareem
Abdul-Jabbar* 41 = David Robinson* 41 **9** Moses Malone* 40

THE TOP 10
Most Field Goals

PLAYER	FIELD GOALS
1 Michael Jordan*	110
2 Kareem Abdul-Jabbar*	105
3 Oscar Robertson*	88
4 Julius Erving*	85
5 Bob Pettit*	81
6 Isiah Thomas*	76
7 John Havlicek*	74
8 Wilt Chamberlain*	72
9 Elgin Baylor*	70
10 Magic Johnson*	64

Kareem Abdul-Jabbar appeared in a record 18 NBA All-Star Games. The 7-2 Hall-of-Fame center holds numerous All-Star records such as most field goals attempted (213), most blocked shots (31), and most personal fouls (57).

THE TOP 10
Most 3-Pt. Field-Goal Attempts

PLAYER	ATTEMPTS
1 = Ray Allen	23
= Gary Payton	23
3 Scottie Pippen	22
4 = Tim Hardaway*	21
= Magic Johnson*	21
= John Stockton*	21
7 = Reggie Miller	19
= Mark Price*	19
9 Kobe Bryant	18
10 Jason Kidd	17

THE TOP 10
Highest Field-Goal Percentages

PLAYER	FGM	FGA	PCT
1 = Larry Nance*	15	21	.714
= Randy Smith*	15	21	.714
3 David Thompson*	33	49	.673
4 Eddie Johnson*	18	28	.643
5 Ralph Sampson*	21	33	.636
6 Paul Westphal*	43	68	.632
7 Anfernee Hardaway*	20	32	.625
8 Artis Gilmore*	18	29	.621
9 Dikembe Mutombo	22	37	.595
10 Rolando Blackman*	29	49	.592

THE TOP 10
Most Three-Point Field Goals

PLAYER	THREE-POINTERS
1 Magic Johnson*	10
2 = Mark Price*	9
= Glen Rice	9
4 = Tim Hardaway*	8
= Jason Kidd	8
6 = Kobe Bryant	7
= Scottie Pippen	7
= John Stockton*	7
9 = Tracy McGrady	6
= Gary Payton	6
= Mitch Richmond*	6
= Isiah Thomas*	6

THE TOP 10
Highest Free-Throw Percentages†

PLAYER	FTM	FTA	PCT
1 = Archie Clark*	11	11	1.000
= Clyde Drexler*	12	12	1.000
= Kevin Garnett	11	11	1.000
= Gary Payton	11	11	1.000
5 Larry Foust*	15	16	.938
6 = Lou Hudson*	14	15	.933
= Don Ohl*	14	15	.933
8 = Magic Johnson*	38	42	.905
= Jerry Lucas*	19	21	.905
10 Adrian Dantley*	17	19	.895

† 10 FTM minimum

MR. ALL-STAR MVP
The East won the 1967 classic over the West, 124-123, thanks in large part to Jerry Lucas' heroics. The Cincinnati Royal scored 25 points, taking home the All-Star Game MVP honors in addition to a cool-looking motorcycle.

NBA.COM FUN FACT
Jerry Lucas won NBA Rookie of the Year honors as a member of the Cincinnati Royals.
Lucas averaged 17.7 points and 17.4 rebounds during the 1963–64 season.

39

THE TOP 10
First NBA Slam-Dunk Winners

YEAR	PLAYER/TEAM
1984	Larry Nance* PHO
1985	Dominique Wilkins* ATL
1986	Spud Webb* ATL
1987	Michael Jordan* CHI
1988	Michael Jordan* CHI
1989	Kenny Walker* NY
1990	Dominique Wilkins* ATL
1991	Dee Brown* BOS
1992	Cedric Ceballos* PHO
1993	Harold Miner* CLE

THE HUMAN HIGHLIGHT FILM

Dominique Wilkins wowed fans for 15 seasons with his high-wire dunking abilities. The 6-8 forward, known for ferocious windmill slams, was one of the most creative dunkers to participate in the annual Slam Dunk contests.

THE TOP 10
First NBA Three-Point Shootout Contest Winners

YEAR	PLAYER/TEAM
1986	Larry Bird* BOS
1987	Larry Bird* BOS
1988	Larry Bird* BOS
1989	Dale Ellis* SEA
1990	Craig Hodges* CHI
1991	Craig Hodges* CHI
1992	Craig Hodges* CHI
1993	Mark Price* CLE
1994	Mark Price* CLE
1995	Glenn Rice MIA

Fittingly, Larry Bird was the first winner of this contest. The Hall-of-Fame forward confirmed why he was the league's best three-point shooter, winning the contest three years in a row.

THE TOP 10
First NBA All-Star Game Results

YEAR	RESULTS/LOCATION
1951	East 111, West 94 (Boston)
1952	East 108, West 91 (Boston)
1953	West 79, East 75 (Fort Wayne, IN)
1954	East 98, West 93 (OT, New York)
1955	East 100, West 91 (New York)
1956	West 108, East 94 (Rochester)
1957	East 109, West 97 (Boston)
1958	East 130, West 118 (St. Louis)
1959	West 124, East 108 (Detroit)
1960	East 125, West 115 (Philadelphia)

The first NBA All-Star Game was held at Boston Garden as 10,094 fans watched the East defeat the West. "Easy" Ed Macauley of the Boston Celtics took MVP honors after scoring a game-high 20 points. He also excelled defensively, holding superstar George Mikan to only four field goals.

THE TOP 10
Last Got Milk? Rookie Challenge Results

YEAR	RESULTS
2003	Sophomores 132, Rookies 112
2002	Rookies 103, Sophomores 97
2001	2000 Rookies 121, 2001 Rookies 113
2000	2000 Rookies 92, 1999 Rookies 81 (OT)
1999	No Game Played
1998	East 85, West 80
1997	East 96, West 91
1996	East 94, West 92
1995	White 83, Green 79 (OT)
1994	Phenoms 74, Sensations 68

Since 2000, the NBA rookies and sophomores have competed on NBA All-Star Saturday (before then it was solely a rookie showdown). Some of the NBA's brightest young players who have competed are Elton Brand, Steve Francis, and Kenyon Martin.

THE TOP 10
Last NBA All-Star Game Results

YEAR	RESULTS/LOCATION
2003	West 155, East 145 (Atlanta)
2002	East 120, West 108 (Philadelphia)
2001	East 111, West 110 (Washington DC)
2000	West 137, East 126 (Oakland)
1999	No Game Played
1998	East 135, West 114 (New York)
1997	East 132, West 120 (Cleveland)
1996	East 129, West 118 (San Antonio)
1995	West 139, East 112 (Phoenix)
1994	East 127, West 118 (Minneapolis)
1993	West 135, East 132 (OT, Salt Lake City)

NBA All-Star Games are always high-scoring affairs. One of the classics occurred at the 2001 All-Star Game. Trailing by 21 points in the fourth quarter, the East roared back and won, thanks to Allen Iverson's 15 points in the last nine minutes.

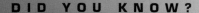

DID YOU KNOW?
Dominique Wilkins has a brother, Gerald, who also played in the NBA. The former guard played for the New York Knicks, Cleveland Cavaliers, Vancouver Grizzlies, and Orlando Magic.

First All-Star Game MVPs

YEAR	PLAYER/TEAM
1951	**Ed Macauley*** BOS
1952	**Paul Arizin*** PHI
1953	**George Mikan*** MIN
1954	**Bob Cousy*** BOS
1955	**Bill Sharman*** BOS
1956	**Bob Pettit*** STL
1957	**Bob Cousy*** BOS
1958	**Bob Pettit*** STL
1959	**Elgin Baylor*** MIN **Bob Pettit*** STL
1960	**Wilt Chamberlain*** PHI

Wilt Chamberlain made a favorable impression in his first NBA All-Star appearance. The 23-year-old rookie scored 23 points and grabbed 25 rebounds in leading the East to a 125-115 win over the West in Philadelphia.

TROPHY PERFORMANCE

It was Michael Jordan's last NBA All-Star Game appearance yet Kevin Garnett walked away with the MVP trophy in the 2003 classic. Garnett shot 17 of 24 from the field and scored 37 points in the West's 155-145 victory in Atlanta.

Last All-Star Game MVPs

YEAR	PLAYER/TEAM
2003	**Kevin Garnett** MIN
2002	**Kobe Bryant** LAL
2001	**Allen Iverson** PHI
2000	**Tim Duncan** SAN **Shaquille O'Neal** LAL
1999	No Game Played
1998	**Michael Jordan*** CHI
1997	**Glen Rice** CHA
1996	**Michael Jordan*** CHI
1995	**Mitch Richmond*** SAS
1994	**Scottie Pippen** CHI
1993	**Karl Malone/John Stockton** UT

Scottie Pippen flourished in his first season without Michael Jordan. In 1994, Pippen dazzled the Minneapolis crowd with his 29-point, 11-rebound performance in the East's victory.

SOARING HAWK

Bob Pettit played in 11 straight NBA All-Star Games and the former Hawk always soared when it came to competing against the league's best players. Pettit earned All-Star Game MVP honors a record four times in 1956, 1958, 1959, and 1962.

THE TOP 10

Nations to Contribute Players to the NBA†

	NATION	PLAYERS
1	Serbia-Montenegro	16
2	Canada	13
3	Croatia	8
4	Germany	7
5=	Australia	5
=	Netherlands	5
=	Puerto Rico	5
8	Many tied with	4

† Other than the United States

The success of Vlade Divac helped pave the way for other players from Serbia and Montenegro to test their skills in the NBA. Drafted by the Los Angeles Lakers with the 26th overall pick in the 1989 NBA Draft, Divac is one of the most versatile centers in the NBA.

THE TOP 10

Alphabetical Order (First)

	PLAYER
1	Alaa Abdelnaby*
2	Zaid Abdul-Aziz*
3	Kareem Abdul-Jabbar*
4	Mahdi Abdul-Rahman†*
5	Mahmoud Abdul-Rauf*
6	Tariq Abdul-Wahad
7	Shareef Abdur-Rahim
8	Tom Abernethy*
9	Forest Able*
10	John Abramovic*

† Also known as Walt Hazzard

Nearly 4,000 players have suited up in the NBA yet the names above are the first 10 listed alphabetically. The first player on the list, Alaa Abdelnaby, played five seasons with five different teams and averaged 5.7 points per game.

THE TOP 10

Alphabetical Order (Last)

	PLAYER
1	Matt Zunic*
2	Bill Zopf*
3	Jim Zoet*
4	George Zidek*
5	Phil Zevenbergen*
6	Tony Zeno*
7	Hank Zeller*
8	Gary Zeller*
9	Dave Zeller*
10	Zeke Zawoluk*

Zeke Zawoluk's place in history is unique: he is the last player listed alphabetically to have played in the NBA. Zeke played a total of three seasons, one with the Indianapolis Jets and two with the Philadelphia Warriors. He averaged 6.8 points per game for his brief career.

THE TOP 10

Father-Son Combined Points

	FATHER	POINTS	SON	POINTS
1	Dolph Schayes*	19,247	Danny Schayes*	8,780
2	Rick Barry*	18,395	Brent Barry*	5,757
3	Rick Barry*	18,395	Jon Barry	3,823
4	Jimmy Walker*	11,655	Jalen Rose	9,708
5	Rick Barry*	18,395	Drew Barry*	134
6	Ernie Vandeweghe*	2,135	Kiki Vandeweghe*	15,980
7	Press Maravich*	412	Pete Maravich*	15,948
8	Joe Bryant*	5,252	Kobe Bryant	10,658
9	Spencer Haywood*	14,592	Brendan Haywood	816
10	Ed Manning*	1,418	Danny Manning*	12,367

THE BARRY FAMILY TREE

Rick Barry (right) scored over 18,000 points in his 10-year career and was selected as one of the 50 Greatest Players in NBA History in 1996. His son, Brent (left), stars for the Seattle SuperSonics and has made his father proud, pouring in nearly 6,000 points in his career. Another son, Jon, plays for the Denver Nuggets, and a third son, Drew, was in the NBA for three years.

THE TOP 10

Tallest Players

PLAYER	HEIGHT
1=Manute Bol*	7-7
=Gheorghe Muresan*	7-7
3 Shawn Bradley	7-6
4=Yao Ming	7-5
=Chuck Nevitt*	7-5
=Slavko Vranes	7-5
7=Mark Eaton*	7-4
=Priest Lauderdale*	7-4
=Ralph Sampson*	7-4
=Rik Smits*	7-4

Three of the tallest players in NBA history—Shawn Bradley, Yao Ming, and Slavko Vranes—currently patrol the center position. Only two of the players on this list—Yao and Ralph Sampson—were selected with the No. 1 overall pick in the NBA Draft.

STANDING TALL
Born in Turalie, Sudan, Manute Bol entered the NBA in 1985. A second-round pick of the Washington Bullets, Bol played 11 seasons with four teams. At 7-7, Bol gave opposing teams fits with his shot-blocking abilities; no one has blocked more shots per minute.

LITTLE BIG MAN
Muggsy Bogues didn't let his diminutive stature deter him from fulfilling his NBA dream. At 5-3, Bogues may have been the shortest player in NBA history but his talent led him to a productive 14-year career. A fan favorite, Bogues played nine seasons with the Hornets.

THE TOP 10

Shortest Players

PLAYER	HEIGHT
1 Muggsy Bogues*	5-3
2 Earl Boykins	5-5
3=Jerry Dover*	5-7
=Greg Grant*	5-7
=Keith Jennings*	5-7
=Herm Klotz*	5-7
=Wat Misaka*	5-7
=Monte Towe*	5-7
=Spud Webb*	5-7
10=Charlie Criss*	5-8
=Mel Hirsch*	5-8

NBA.COM FUN FACT
Manute Bol owns the second highest single-game record for most blocks with 15.
He did it twice as a member of the Washington Bullets.

43

Regular-Season Attendance

	LOCATION	DATE	PEOPLE
1	CHI at ATL (Georgia Dome)	3/27/98	62,046
2	BOS at DET (Silverdome)	1/29/88	61,983
3	PHI at DET (Silverdome)	2/14/87	52,745
4	DEN at MIN (Metrodome)	4/17/90	49,551
5	ATL at DET (Silverdome)	3/30/88	47,692
6	CHI at ATL (Georgia Dome)	11/7/97	45,790
7	ORL at MIN (Metrodome)	4/13/90	45,458
8	ATL at DET (Silverdome)	2/21/87	44,970
9	PHI at DET (Silverdome)	2/15/86	44,180
10	PHI at DET (Silverdome)	2/16/85	43,816

A BULLISH GATHERING

The Bulls were always a top road draw during the Michael Jordan–era in Chicago, especially during his last season in the Windy City. In the team's final appearance in Atlanta, the Hawks accommodated the huge ticket demand and moved their home game from The Omni to the spacious Georgia Dome. More than 62,000 fans watched the Bulls defeat the Hawks 89-74.

All-Star Attendance

	LOCATION	DATE	PEOPLE
1	**Astrodome,** Houston, TX	2/12/89	44,735
2	**Hoosier Dome,** Indianapolis, IN	2/10/85	43,146
3	**Alamodome,** San Antonio, TX	2/11/96	36,037
4	**Kingdome,** Seattle, WA	2/8/87	34,275
5	**Silverdome,** St. Louis, MI	2/4/79	31,745
6	**Charlotte Coliseum,** Charlotte, NC	2/10/91	23,530
7	**Gund Arena,** Cleveland, OH	2/9/97	20,592
8	**MCI Center,** Washington, DC	2/11/01	20,374
9	**Philips Arena,** Atlanta, GA	2/9/03	20,325
10	**The Coliseum,** Memphis, TN	2/1/81	20,239

A record crowd saw Karl Malone lead the West to a 143-134 victory over the East at the Astrodome. The Mailman scored 28 points and grabbed nine rebounds, while his teammate John Stockton started in place of the injured Magic Johnson. Stockton scored 11 points, dished 17 assists, and five steals.

DID YOU KNOW?
In his final season in Chicago, Michael Jordan led the NBA in scoring with a 28.7 scoring average, earned NBA MVP honors, and guided the Bulls to the 1998 NBA championship.

HOOPS HEAVEN

The Naismith Memorial Basketball Hall of Fame is the ultimate state-of-the-art interactive museum. Located in Springfield, Massachusetts, the birthplace of basketball, this 80,000-square-foot facility, which opened its doors in 2002, honors the game's greatest teams, players, and contributors.

Named after the game's founder, Dr. James Naismith, this is the third building the Hall of Fame has called home. The first Hall was born on Springfield College's campus on February 17, 1968. Soon the exhibits outgrew the space, and a new Hall opened in Springfield's business district on June 30, 1985.

In this new basketball-shaped Hall, fans can test their skills at various interactive exhibits, check out the countless memorabilia on display, relive old game footage, or shoot hoops at center court on a multitude  of baskets, ranging from peach baskets to glass backboards. Inside the dome is the Honors Ring, which features more than 250 members.

THE TOP 10

Arena Capacities

	ARENA	TEAM	PEOPLE
1	The Palace of Auburn Hills	DET	22,076
2	United Center	CHI	21,711
3	MCI Center	WAS	20,674
4	Gund Arena	CLE	20,562
5	First Union Center	PHI	20,444
6	Continental Airlines Arena	NJ	20,049
7	The Rose Garden	POR	19,980
8	Delta Center	UT	19,911
9	Air Canada Centre	TOR	19,800
10	Madison Square Garden	NY	19,763

The Palace of Auburn Hills debuted on November 5, 1988, when the Detroit Pistons hosted the Charlotte Hornets. The Pistons notched their first-ever win that night at the new state-of-the-art arena, defeating the Hornets 94-85. It was the start of something special as the Pistons went on to win the NBA championship later that season.

THE TOP 10

First Players Inducted into the Hall of Fame

YEAR	PLAYER
1959	George Mikan*
1960	Ed Macauley*
1961	Andy Phillip*
1970	Bob Davies*
1971	Bob Cousy*/Bob Pettit*
1973	Dolph Schayes*
1975	Bill Russell*
1976	Tom Gola*/Bill Sharman*

The Basketball Hall of Fame inducted its first class in 1959, which was nine years before the doors officially opened. A total of 17 inductees were honored that year, including NBA superstar George Mikan of the Minneapolis Lakers, while the barnstorming Original Celtics were the first great team to be enshrined.

THE TOP 10

Teams with the Most Players in the Hall of Fame

	TEAM	PLAYERS
1	Boston Celtics	29
2	Los Angeles Lakers	17
3	Golden State Warriors	16
4=	Atlanta Hawks	15
=	Detroit Pistons	15
=	New York Knicks	15
7=	Philadelphia 76ers	13
=	Sacramento Kings	13
9	Washington Wizards	9
10	New Jersey Nets	8

The Celtics own the most NBA championships in NBA history with 16. So it isn't surprising that the franchise also boasts the most representatives in the Hall of Fame, with 29.

NBA PLAYOFFS

MARQUEE MATCHUP

The Boston Celtics–Philadelphia 76ers rivalry was legendary in the 1960s and continued to grow in the '80s. Julius Erving and the Sixers faced Larry Bird and the Celtics in the Eastern Conference Finals four times in a six-year period.

THE TOP 10

Highest Scoring Averages†

	PLAYER	G	FGM	FTM	PTS	AVG
1	Allen Iverson	57	618	404	1,743	30.6
2	Shaquille O'Neal	136	1,476	869	3,821	28.1
3	Karl Malone	172	1,645	1,223	4,519	26.3
4	Paul Pierce	26	199	221	665	25.6
5	Dirk Nowitzki	35	292	251	891	25.5
6=	Ray Allen	26	223	107	629	24.2
=	Tim Duncan	72	637	463	1,739	24.2
8	Reggie Miller	115	834	675	2,618	22.8
9	Kobe Bryant	97	79	500	2,155	22.2
10	Chris Webber	47	422	169	1,021	21.7

† 25 games or 625 points minimum

Allen Iverson continues to amaze, especially in the postseason. His many spectacular playoff moments include the feat he performed in the first round of the 2003 NBA Playoffs, when he dropped 55 points on the New Orleans Hornets, which set a single-game franchise postseason mark.

INSTANT OFFENSE

Ever since he entered the NBA in 1998, Paul Pierce has been a scoring force. The 6-6 forward averaged 25 or more points in the last three seasons and has also maintained that scoring touch in the postseason, averaging 25.6 points per game.

THE TOP 10

Most Points

	PLAYER	POINTS
1	Karl Malone	4,519
2	Shaquille O'Neal	3,821
3	Scottie Pippen	3,642
4	Reggie Miller	2,618
5	Kobe Bryant	2,155
6	Horace Grant	1,907
7	Gary Payton	1,779
8	Allen Iverson	1,743
9	Tim Duncan	1,739
10	Robert Horry	1,509

Karl Malone has always elevated his game during the playoffs. In 18 postseason appearances as a member of the Utah Jazz, Malone has averaged 26.3 points per game, which is slightly better than his career regular season average of 25.4.

THE TOP 10

Most Field Goals

	PLAYER	FIELD GOALS
1	Karl Malone	1,645
2	Shaquille O'Neal	1,476
3	Scottie Pippen	1,335
4	Reggie Miller	834
5	Horace Grant	786
6	Kobe Bryant	779
7	Gary Payton	705
8	Tim Duncan	637
9	Allen Iverson	618
10	Robert Horry	525

Gary Payton is the lone point guard to place among the top 10 active players on this list. The Los Angeles Lakers' point guard can fill it up with the best of them. Payton has averaged more than 17.8 points per game during his 13-year career.

THE TOP 10

Most Free Throws

	PLAYER	FREE THROWS
1	Karl Malone	1,223
2	Shaquille O'Neal	869
3	Scottie Pippen	772
4	Reggie Miller	675
5	Kobe Bryant	500
6	Tim Duncan	463
7	Allen Iverson	404
8	Vlade Divac	356
9	Alonzo Mourning	340
10	Horace Grant	334

In his first postseason series as a rookie, Shaquille O'Neal shot .471 from the free-throw line. Since then, Shaq has improved his accuracy by consistently raising his average to a personal best of .649, which he reached during the 2002 NBA Playoffs.

DID YOU KNOW?

Paul Pierce led the NBA in points scored with 2,144 during the 2001–02 season.

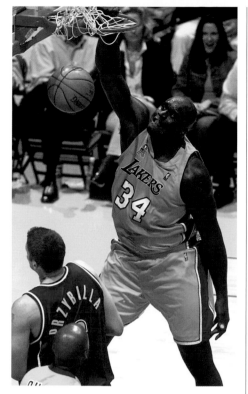

UNSTOPPABLE FORCE

How do you stop a 7-1, 300-plus pound All-Star center? You don't, especially when he has the ball under the basket. Shaquille O'Neal's ability to secure great low-post position presents him with many high-percentage shots.

THE TOP 10

Highest Field-Goal Percentages†

	PLAYER	FGM	FGA	PCT
1	Shaquille O'Neal	1,476	2,644	.558
2	Dale Davis	337	615	.548
3	Horace Grant	786	1,483	.530
4	Anthony Mason	333	636	.524
5	Dikembe Mutombo	284	553	.514
6	Tim Duncan	637	1,261	.505
7=	Alonzo Mourning	374	769	.486
=	Avery Johnson	398	819	.486
9	Kevin Willis	395	815	.485
10	Scott Williams	201	415	.484

† 150 FGM minimum

THE TOP 10

Highest 3-Pt. Field-Goal Percentages†

	PLAYER	3FGM	3FGA	PCT
1	Ray Allen	76	164	.463
2	Steve Nash	75	169	.444
3	Tim Thomas	39	89	.438
4	Derek Fisher	121	279	.434
5	Keith Van Horn	51	118	.432
6	Tony Delk	47	110	.427
7	Rasheed Wallace	40	95	.421
8	Allan Houston	76	181	.420
9	Eddie Jones	67	160	.419
10	Dirk Nowitzki	56	135	.415

† 35 3FGM minimum

The lone seven footer on this list, Dallas Maverick Dirk Nowitzki from Wurzburg, Germany, is a great shooter who possesses terrific range. Leave him open or give him a clean look from three-point territory and it's an automatic basket.

The Top 10 Most Three-Point Field Goals

Player/Three-Pointers

① **Reggie Miller** 275 **②** **Scottie Pippen** 200 **③** **Robert Horry** 191 **④** **Bryon Russell** 126 **⑤** **Derek Fisher** 121 **⑥** **Nick Van Exel** 111 **⑦** **Gary Payton** 105 **⑧** **Allen Iverson** 103 **⑨** **Toni Kukoc** 99 **⑩** **Kobe Bryant** 97

It shouldn't come as a surprise that Reggie Miller tops the list of most three-pointers made. The NBA's all-time regular-season leader has produced many dramatic clutch playoff highlights from the three-point line.

PEJA STOJAKOVIC

Predrag Stojakovic is one of the best shooters in the NBA. The 6-9 forward from Serbia-Montenegro has not only won the NBA's three-point contest multiple times but he is an excellent free-throw shooter as well.

THE TOP 10

Highest Free-Throw Percentages†

	PLAYER	FTM	FTA	PCT
1	Richard Hamilton	106	117	.906
2	Pedrag Stojakovic	155	173	.896
3	Dirk Nowitzki	251	281	.893
4	Reggie Miller	675	760	.888
5	Steve Nash	124	140	.886
6=	Allan Houston	268	303	.884
=	Ray Allen	107	121	.884
8	Michael Finley	138	160	.863
9	Sam Cassell	288	337	.855
10	Glen Rice	169	200	.845

† 100 FTM minimum

THE TOP 10

Most Games Played

PLAYER	GAMES
1 Scottie Pippen	208
2 Karl Malone	172
3 Horace Grant	170
4 Robert Horry	165
5 Charles Oakley	144
6 Shaquille O'Neal	136
7 Mark Jackson	126
8 Clifford Robinson	125
9 Vlade Divac	109
10 Dale Davis	108

Karl Malone will continue to climb the active leaders' chart for games played in the playoffs as a member of the Los Angeles Lakers. The 6-9 power forward has had plenty of experience as a member of the Utah Jazz.

THE TOP 10

Most Minutes Played

PLAYER	MINUTES
1 Scottie Pippen	8,105
2 Karl Malone	7,109
3 Horace Grant	6,172
4 Shaquille O'Neal	5,465
5 Robert Horry	5,255
6 Charles Oakley	5,108
7 Reggie Miller	4,423
8 Mark Jackson	3,737
9 Clifford Robinson	3,598
10 Kobe Bryant	3,583

BEAM ME UP

Scottie Pippen rose to the top of the active leaders' chart for most playoff games played, thanks to the Bulls' glorious championship run in the 1990s. Pippen racked up 177 games, which included six NBA Finals appearances, during his first 11 seasons in the league.

THE TOP 10

Most Offensive Rebounds

PLAYER	OFFENSIVE REBOUNDS
1 Shaquille O'Neal	631
2 Horace Grant	549
3 Charles Oakley	519
4 Scottie Pippen	466
5 Karl Malone	465
6 Dale Davis	346
7 Shawn Kemp	314
8 Robert Horry	292
9 Vlade Divac	285
10 Dikembe Mutombo	265

Footwork, positioning, balance—those are just some of the skills to being a good rebounder. Size also helps. Los Angeles Laker Shaquille O'Neal has all of the above as he has emerged as the active leader for most rebounds in the NBA Playoffs.

THE TOP 10

Most Defensive Rebounds

PLAYER	DEFENSIVE REBOUNDS
1 Karl Malone	1,412
2 Shaquille O'Neal	1,118
3 Scottie Pippen	1,117
4 Charles Oakley	926
5 Horace Grant	908
6 Robert Horry	731
7 Tim Duncan	710
8 Dale Davis	643
9 Dikembe Mutombo	593
10 Vlade Divac	569

Now that he has rejoined the Chicago Bulls, Scottie Pippen hopes to add to his defensive rebounding totals in the postseason. Pippen played for the Bulls the last time they made the playoffs in 1998. The six-time champion (all while a member of the Bulls) plans on leading Chicago to a few more postseason appearances before he retires.

THE TOP 10
Most Rebounds Total

	PLAYER	REBOUNDS
1	Karl Malone	1,877
2	Shaquille O'Neal	1,749
3	Scottie Pippen	1,583
4	Horace Grant	1,457
5	Charles Oakley	1,445
6	Robert Horry	1,023
7	Dale Davis	989
8	Tim Duncan	963
9	Dikembe Mutombo	858
10	Vlade Divac	854

Look for Tim Duncan to climb the rebounding postseason charts for years to come. The five-time NBA All-Star averages over 15 boards per game.

DEFENSIVE PRESENCE

For more than 15 seasons, Horace Grant developed the reputation as one of the NBA's better defensive power forwards. Grant is a four-time member of the NBA's All-Defensive Second Team and has averaged more than eight rebounds per game throughout his career.

THE GLOVE

Gary Payton has proven that he is one of the all-time great NBA point guards. Starring in Seattle for 12-plus seasons, he climbed his way up the franchise's all-time assists and steals lists, and is nicknamed "The Glove" for his ability to swarm an opponent.

THE TOP 10
Most Assists

	PLAYER	ASSISTS
1	Scottie Pippen	1,048
2	Mark Jackson	900
3	Gary Payton	624
4=	Avery Johnson	562
=	Jason Kidd	562
6	Karl Malone	538
7	Robert Horry	471
8	Shaquille O'Neal	437
9	Sam Cassell	428
10	Kobe Bryant	407

The greatness of Shaquille O'Neal isn't limited to scoring and rebounding, he is also an excellent passer. Shaq is often double-teamed by opponents, which leads to passes to teammates on the perimeter, translating into easy baskets.

THE TOP 10
Most Blocked Shots

	PLAYER	BLOCKS
1	Shaquille O'Neal	313
2	Dikembe Mutombo	224
3	Tim Duncan	221
4	Scottie Pippen	185
5	Horace Grant	173
6	Robert Horry	165
7	Greg Ostertag	163
8	Vlade Divac	160
9	Alonzo Mourning	155
10	Shawn Kemp	137

Robert Horry is nicknamed "Big Shot Rob" for his ability to nail clutch perimeter baskets in the playoffs. He also ranks sixth in shot-blocking.

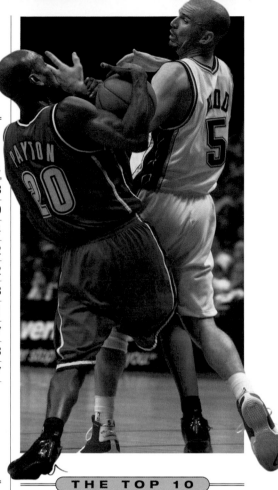

THE TOP 10
Most Steals

	PLAYER	STEALS
1	Scottie Pippen	395
2	Karl Malone	234
3	Robert Horry	226
4	Charles Oakley	178
5	Horace Grant	171
6	Gary Payton	164
7	Mark Jackson	129
8	Clifford Robinson	128
9	Allen Iverson	126
10	Jason Kidd	121

The Chicago Bulls' Scottie Pippen and Michael Jordan formed a devastating defensive one-two punch in the playoffs. A lot of Pippen's steals have been a result of hard work and double teams during Chicago's championship runs.

NBA.COM FUN FACT

Scottie Pippen was originally drafted by the Seattle SuperSonics in 1987. The Bulls traded their first-round pick, forward/center Olden Polynice, plus a future second-round pick for Pippen.

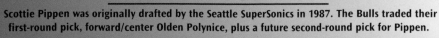

51

CLUTCH PERFORMER

In didn't take Allen Iverson long to establish himself as one of the greatest scorers in NBA Playoff history. Iverson ranks second only to Michael Jordan in playoffs scoring average. The 2001 NBA MVP will look to challenge that top spot for years to come.

THE TOP 10
Highest Scoring Averages†

	PLAYER	G	FGM	FTM	PTS	AVG
1	Michael Jordan*	179	2,188	1,463	5,987	33.4
2	Allen Iverson	57	618	404	1,743	30.6
3	Jerry West*	153	1,622	1,213	4,457	29.1
4	Shaquille O'Neal	136	1,476	869	3,821	28.1
5=	Elgin Baylor*	134	1,388	847	3,623	27.0
=	George Gervin*	59	622	348	1,592	27.0
7	Karl Malone	172	1,645	1,223	4,519	26.3
8	Hakeem Olajuwon*	145	1,504	743	3,755	25.9
9	Paul Pierce	26	199	221	665	25.6
10	Dirk Nowitzki	35	292	251	891	25.5

† 25 games or 625 points minimum

The Top 10 Leading Scorers

Player/Points

1 Michael Jordan* 5,987 **2** Kareem Abdul-Jabbar* 5,762
3 Karl Malone 4,519 **4** Jerry West* 4,457 **5** Larry Bird* 3,897
6 Shaquille O'Neal 3,821 **7** John Havlicek* 3,776
8 Hakeem Olajuwon* 3,755 **9** Magic Johnson* 3,701
10 Scottie Pippen 3,642

THE TOP 10
Most Three-Point Field Goals

	PLAYER	THREE-POINTERS
1	Reggie Miller	275
2	Scottie Pippen	200
3	Robert Horry	191
4	Dan Majerle*	181
5	John Starks*	176
6	Danny Ainge*	172
7	Sam Perkins*	152
8	Terry Porter*	151
9	Michael Jordan*	148
10	Clyde Drexler*	141

John Starks was a valuable member of the New York Knicks during their title pursuit in the 1990s. He loved to let it fly from three-point land.

THE TOP 10
Highest 3-Pt. Field-Goal Percentages†

	PLAYER	3FGM	3FGA	PCT
1	Bob Hansen*	38	76	.500
2	Ray Allen	76	164	.463
3	B. J. Armstrong*	51	113	.451
4	Kenny Smith*	117	261	.448
5	Steve Nash	75	169	.444
6	Tim Thomas	39	89	.438
7	Derek Fisher	121	279	.434
8	Jeff Hornacek*	122	282	.433
9	Keith Van Horn	51	118	.432
10	Tony Delk	47	110	.427

† 35 3FGM minimum

THE TOP 10
Most Field Goals

	PLAYER	FIELD GOALS
1	Kareem Abdul-Jabbar*	2,356
2	Michael Jordan*	2,188
3	Karl Malone	1,645
4	Jerry West*	1,622
5	Hakeem Olajuwon*	1,504
6	Shaquille O'Neal	1,476
7	Larry Bird*	1,458
8	John Havlicek*	1,451
9	Wilt Chamberlain*	1,425
10	Elgin Baylor*	1,388

Only two players in NBA Playoff history have scored 2,000 or more field goals—Kareem Abdul-Jabbar and Michael Jordan. It also isn't a coincidence that both rank at the top of the all-time Playoff scoring charts.

DID YOU KNOW?
Allen Iverson shares the record for most free throws made in a quarter with nine. He did it in Game 3 of the 2001 NBA Finals versus the Los Angeles Lakers.

LOW-POST DOMINATOR

Whenever Kevin McHale received the ball near the basket, opposing teams were defenseless. The 6-10 power forward was virtually unstoppable when scoring. McHale's long arms and array of moves aided him in shooting .561 percent from the field.

THE TOP 10

Highest Field-Goal Percentages†

	PLAYER	FGM	FGA	PCT
1	James Donaldson*	153	244	.627
2	Kurt Rambis*	284	495	.574
3	Otis Thorpe*	321	564	.569
4	Artis Gilmore*	179	315	.568
5	Mark West*	201	355	.566
6	Kevin McHale*	1,204	2,145	.561
7	Bernard King*	269	481	.559
8	Shaquille O'Neal	1,476	2,644	.558
9	Dale Davis	337	615	.548
10	Darryl Dawkins*	542	992	.546

† 150 FGM minimum

THE TOP 10

Most Free Throws

	PLAYER	FREE THROWS
1	Michael Jordan*	1,463
2	Karl Malone	1,223
3	Jerry West*	1,213
4	Magic Johnson*	1,068
5	Kareem Abdul-Jabbar*	1,050
6	Larry Bird*	901
7	John Havlicek*	874
8	Shaquille O'Neal	869
9	Elgin Baylor*	847
10	Scottie Pippen	772

Not only did Michael Jordan have the knack for getting to the free-throw line but he also netted a high percentage from there as well. The six-time NBA Finals MVP shot .828 percent from the line during the playoffs and ranks No. 1 all-time with 1,463 free throws made.

ON THE MARK

Mark Price was always on target when it came to free-throw shooting. The point guard shot .904 percent from the line during his career and improved upon that number during the NBA Playoffs with .944. Price played 12 years in the NBA, nine in Cleveland.

THE TOP 10

Highest Free-Throw Percentages†

	PLAYER	FTM	FTA	PCT
1	Mark Price*	202	214	.944
2	Calvin Murphy*	165	177	.932
3	Bill Sharman*	370	406	.911
4=	Kiki Vandeweghe*	235	259	.907
=	Hersey Hawkins*	292	322	.907
6	Richard Hamilton	106	117	.906
7	Predrag Stojakovic	155	173	.896
8	Dirk Nowitzki	251	281	.893
9	Larry Bird*	901	1,012	.890
10	Vince Boryla*	120	135	.889

† 100 FTM minimum

THE TOP 10

Most Games Played

PLAYER	GAMES
1 Kareem Abdul-Jabbar*	237
2 Scottie Pippen	208
3 Danny Ainge*	193
4 Magic Johnson*	190
5 Robert Parish*	184
6 Byron Scott*	183
7 John Stockton*	182
8 Dennis Johnson*	180
9 Michael Jordan*	179
10=John Havlicek*	172
=Karl Malone	172

KING KAREEM

Kareem Abdul-Jabbar played in 20 NBA seasons, including 18 postseason appearances, which is an NBA record. Abdul-Jabbar posted virutally the same scoring average in the playoffs (24.3) as he did in the regular season (24.6).

THE TOP 10

Most Minutes Played

PLAYER	MINUTES
1 Kareem Abdul-Jabbar*	8,851
2 Scottie Pippen	8,105
3 Wilt Chamberlain*	7,559
4 Magic Johnson*	7,538
5 Bill Russell*	7,497
6 Michael Jordan*	7,474
7 Karl Malone	7,109
8 Dennis Johnson*	6,994
9 Larry Bird*	6,886
10 John Havlicek*	6,860

Kareem Abdul-Jabbar averaged 37.3 minutes per contest in 18 seasons of postseason play. The six-time NBA MVP played five of those seasons with the Milwaukee Bucks, which he led to the 1971 NBA championship. Abdul-Jabbar also earned 1971 NBA Finals MVP honors.

THE TOP 10

Most Defensive Rebounds

PLAYER	DEFENSIVE REBOUNDS
1 Karl Malone	1,412
2 Larry Bird*	1,323
3 Kareem Abdul-Jabbar*	1,273
4 Robert Parish*	1,194
5 Hakeem Olajuwon*	1,150
6 Shaquille O'Neal	1,118
7 Scottie Pippen	1,117
8 Magic Johnson*	1,116
9 Patrick Ewing*	1,098
10 Charles Barkley*	1,072

Karl Malone played 18 seasons in Utah and led the Jazz to two back-to-back NBA Finals appearances in 1997 and '98. Malone and the Jazz never missed the postseason during his career in Salt Lake City. The Mailman also delivers more rebounds in the postseason (11.0) than he does in the regular season (10.3).

THE TOP 10

Most Offensive Rebounds

PLAYER	OFFENSIVE REBOUNDS
1 Shaquille O'Neal	631
2 Dennis Rodman*	626
3 Robert Parish*	571
4 Horace Grant	549
5 Charles Oakley	519
6=Charles Barkley*	510
=Moses Malone*	510
8 Kareem Abdul-Jabbar*	505
9 Hakeem Olajuwon*	471
10 Scottie Pippen	466

Shaquille O'Neal rises to the occasion in the postseason, averaging more points, rebounds, and assists in the playoffs than he does in the regular season. His offensive rebounding numbers are also higher in the playoffs (4.5) than the regular season (3.9).

THE TOP 10

Most Rebounds Total

PLAYER	REBOUNDS
1 Bill Russell*	4,104
2 Wilt Chamberlain*	3,913
3 Kareem Abdul-Jabbar*	2,481
4 Karl Malone	1,877
5 Wes Unseld*	1,777
6 Robert Parish*	1,765
7 Shaquille O'Neal	1,749
8 Elgin Baylor*	1,724
9 Larry Bird*	1,683
10 Dennis Rodman*	1,676

LARRY LEGEND

The all-around brilliance of Larry Bird is reflected in the various number of postseason categories in which his name appears. He shows up in the top 10 of minutes, rebounds, assists, and steals. Bird helped lead the Boston Celtics to three NBA championships.

THE TOP 10
Most Assists

	PLAYER	ASSISTS
1	Magic Johnson*	2,346
2	John Stockton*	1,839
3	Larry Bird*	1,062
4	Scottie Pippen	1,048
5	Michael Jordan*	1,022
6	Dennis Johnson*	1,006
7	Isiah Thomas*	987
8	Jerry West*	970
9	Bob Cousy*	937
10	Kevin Johnson*	935

THE TOP 10
Most Steals

	PLAYER	STEALS
1	Scottie Pippen	395
2	Michael Jordan*	376
3	Magic Johnson*	358
4	John Stockton*	338
5	Larry Bird*	296
6	Maurice Cheeks*	295
7	Clyde Drexler*	278
8	Dennis Johnson*	247
9	Hakeem Olajuwon*	245
10	Julius Erving*	235

RETURN TO SENDER

Hakeem Olajuwon shares several postseason shot-blocking records including the single-game playoff record with 10 and the NBA Finals single-game record with 8. He led the Houston Rockets to back-to-back NBA titles in 1994 and '95.

THE TOP 10
Most Blocked Shots

	PLAYER	BLOCKS
1	Kareem Abdul-Jabbar*	476
2	Hakeem Olajuwon*	472
3	Shaquille O'Neal	313
4	David Robinson*	312
5	Robert Parish*	309
6	Patrick Ewing*	303
7	Kevin McHale*	281
8	Julius Erving*	239
9	Dikembe Mutombo	224
10	Caldwell Jones*	223

NBA.COM FUN FACT
Larry Bird led the Boston Celtics to five NBA Finals appearances in the 1980s, and he is a two-time Finals MVP winner (1984 and '86).

55

Most Points

	PLAYER/TEAM	DATE	FG	FT	PTS
1	**Michael Jordan*** CHI	4/20/86	22	19	63
2	**Elgin Baylor*** LAL	4/14/62	22	17	61
3=	**Wilt Chamberlain*** PHI	3/22/62	22	12	56
=	**Michael Jordan*** CHI	4/29/92	20	16	56
=	**Charles Barkley*** PHO	5/4/94	23	7	56
6=	**Rick Barry*** SF	4/18/67	22	11	55
=	**Michael Jordan*** CHI	5/1/88	24	7	55
=	**Michael Jordan*** CHI	6/16/93	21	13	55
=	**Michael Jordan*** CHI	4/27/97	22	10	55
=	**Allen Iverson** PHI	4/20/03	21	10	55

In Game 2 of the First Round of the 1986 NBA Playoffs, Michael Jordan rocked the Boston Garden, scoring 63 points in only his second season in the NBA. Despite his heroics, the Bulls lost to the Boston Celtics in a triple-overtime thriller, 135-131.

PASSIONATE COMPETITOR

Rick Barry has the unique distinction of being the only player to ever lead the NCAA, ABA, and NBA in scoring. An eight-time NBA All-Star, Barry led the league in scoring in only his second season with the San Francisco Warriors, averaging 35.6 points per game.

Most Field Goals

	PLAYER/TEAM	DATE	FGM	FGA
1=	**Wilt Chamberlain*** PHI	3/14/60	24	42
=	**John Havlicek*** BOS	4/1/73	24	36
=	**Michael Jordan*** CHI	5/1/88	24	45
4	**Charles Barkley*** PHO	5/4/94	23	31
5=	**Wilt Chamberlain*** PHI	3/22/60	22	42
=	**Wilt Chamberlain*** PHI	3/22/62	22	48
=	**Elgin Baylor*** LAL	4/14/62	22	46
=	**Wilt Chamberlain*** SF	4/10/64	22	32
=	**Rick Barry*** SF	4/18/67	22	48
=	**Billy Cunningham*** PHI	4/1/70	22	39
=	**Michael Jordan*** CHI	4/20/86	22	41
=	**Michael Jordan*** CHI	4/27/97	22	35

Nicknamed "The Kangaroo Kid" for his extraordinary jumping ability, Billy Cunningham was one of the premier players of his era. The 6-7 forward averaged 20.8 points during his 10-year career with the Philadelphia 76ers.

DID YOU KNOW?
Rick Barry was named MVP of the 1975 NBA Finals when he led the Golden State Warriors to a four-game upset sweep of the Washington Bullets.

Most Free Throws

	PLAYER/TEAM	DATE	FTM	FTA
1	**Bob Cousy*** BOS	3/21/53	30	32
2	**Michael Jordan*** CHI	5/14/89	23	28
3=	**Michael Jordan*** CHI	5/5/89	22	27
=	**Karl Malone** UT	5/3/92	22	24
5=	**Oscar Robertson*** CIN	4/10/63	21	22
=	**Derrick Coleman** NJ	5/6/94	21	25
=	**Kevin Johnson*** PHO	5/20/95	21	22
=	**Paul Pierce** BOS	4/19/03	21	21
9=	**Bob Cousy*** BOS	3/17/54	20	25
=	**Jerry West*** LAL	4/3/62	20	23
=	**Jerry West*** LAL	4/5/65	20	21
=	**Magic Johnson*** LAL	5/8/91	20	22
=	**Karl Malone** UT	5/9/91	20	22

Hall-of-Fame point guard Bob Cousy of the Boston Celtics excelled from the free-throw line. Cousy nailed 30 of 32 free throws in Game 2 of the 1953 Eastern Division Semifinals. The 13-time All-Star's free-throw shooting helped Boston secure a 111-105 quadruple-overtime win against the Syracuse Nationals.

Most Steals

	PLAYER/TEAM	DATE	STEALS
1=	**Allen Iverson** PHI	5/13/99	8
=	**Rick Barry*** GS	4/14/75	8
=	**Lionel Hollins*** POR	5/8/77	8
=	**Maurice Cheeks*** PHI	4/11/79	8
=	**Craig Hodges*** MIL	5/9/86	8
=	**Tim Hardaway*** GS	5/8/91	8
=	**Tim Hardaway*** GS	4/30/92	8
=	**Mookie Blaylock*** ATL	4/29/96	8
9	**Many tied with**		7

Often overshadowed by his higher profile teammates Julius Erving, Moses Malone, and Charles Barkley, Maurice Cheeks established himself as one of the greatest point guards of his era, playing 11 seasons in Philadelphia. Cheeks swiped eight steals versus the New Jersey Nets in Game 1 of the 1979 NBA Playoffs.

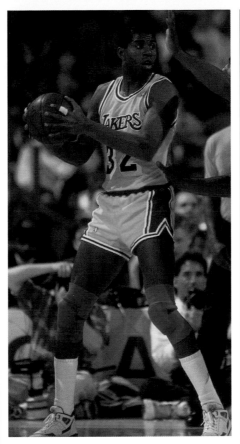

LENDING A HAND

Few rose to the occasion like Laker Magic Johnson come playoff time. The do-everything guard guided Los Angeles to five NBA titles in the 1980s. Magic was an assist machine during the postseason and retired as the then NBA's all-time assists leader.

Most Assists

	PLAYER/TEAM	DATE	ASSISTS
1=	**Magic Johnson*** LAL	5/15/84	24
=	**John Stockton*** UT	5/17/88	24
3=	**Magic Johnson*** LAL	5/3/85	23
=	**John Stockton*** UT	4/25/96	23
5	**Doc Rivers*** ATL	5/16/88	22
6=	**Magic Johnson*** LAL	6/3/84	21
=	**Magic Johnson*** LAL	4/27/91	21
=	**Magic Johnson*** LAL	5/18/91	21
=	**John Stockton*** UT	4/24/92	21
10	**Many tied with**		20

Most Rebounds

	PLAYER/TEAM	DATE	REB.
1	**Wilt Chamberlain*** PHI	4/5/67	41
2=	**Bill Russell*** BOS	3/23/58	40
=	**Bill Russell*** BOS	3/29/60	40
=	**Bill Russell*** BOS	4/18/62	40
5=	**Bill Russell*** BOS	3/19/60	39
=	**Bill Russell*** BOS	3/23/61	39
=	**Wilt Chamberlain*** PHI	4/6/65	39
8=	**Bill Russell*** BOS	4/11/61	38
=	**Bill Russell*** BOS	4/16/63	38
=	**Wilt Chamberlain*** SF	4/24/64	38
=	**Wilt Chamberlain*** PHI	4/16/67	38

The totals appear unfathomable: 41 rebounds in a single game in the playoffs? Evidenced by the Top 10 list, it was rather routine for superstars Wilt Chamberlain and Bill Russell to control the boards during the postseason. The hard work paid off. Chamberlain and the Philadelphia 76ers won the NBA title in 1967, and Russell and the Celtics won 11 titles in 13 seasons.

Most Blocked Shots

	PLAYER/TEAM	DATE	BLOCKS
1=	**Mark Eaton*** UT	4/26/85	10
=	**Hakeem Olajuwon*** HOU	4/29/90	10
3=	**Kareem Abdul-Jabbar*** LAL	4/22/77	9
=	**Manute Bol*** WAS	4/18/86	9
=	**Hakeem Olajuwon*** HOU	4/29/93	9
=	**Derrick Coleman** NJ	5/7/93	9
=	**Greg Ostertag** UT	5/12/97	9
=	**Alonzo Mourning** MIA	4/22/00	9
9	**Many tied with**		8

At 6-10, Alonzo Mourning is considered undersized at the center position. Regardless, Zo has proven to be one of the premier players of his era, once blocking nine shots in a single playoff game. He remains the franchise leader for the New Orleans Hornets in blocked shots.

BALTIMORE'S FINEST

The Baltimore Bullets won the second-ever NBA championship by defeating the Philadelphia Warriors in six games in the 1948 NBA Finals. Kleggie Hermsen (second from left) led the team in scoring that season.

THE TOP 10

All-Time Overall Records

	TEAM	W	L	PCT
1	**Los Angeles Lakers**	366	241	.603
2	**Boston Celtics**	285	202	.585
3	**Chicago Bulls**	147	106	.581
4	**Baltimore Bullets***	9	7	.563
5	**Philadelphia 76ers**	203	183	.526
6	**New York Knicks**	179	171	.511
7	**San Antonio Spurs**	99	97	.505
8	**Houston Rockets**	100	99	.503
9=	**Anderson Packers***	4	4	.500
=	**Indiana Pacers**	63	63	.500

THE TOP 10

All-Time Series Records

	TEAM	W	L	PCT
1	**Boston Celtics**	66	27	.710
2	**Los Angeles Lakers**	90	37	.709
3	**Anderson Packers***	2	1	.667
4	**Chicago Bulls**	34	18	.654
5	**Baltimore Bullets***	3	2	.600
6	**New York Knicks**	40	34	.541
7	**Houston Rockets**	22	19	.537
8	**Philadelphia 76ers**	42	39	.519
9	**Seattle SuperSonics**	21	20	.512
10	**San Antonio Spurs**	20	21	.488

It isn't a surprise that the Boston Celtics rank No. 1 all time in boasting the best NBA Playoff series record at 66-27. After all, the Celtics have won an NBA-record 16 championship titles. The franchise has only missed making the playoffs 14 times in the NBA's 57 years of existence.

THE TOP 10

All-Time Road Records

	TEAM	W	L	PCT
1	**Los Angeles Lakers**	130	159	.450
2	**Boston Celtics**	95	132	.419
3	**Chicago Bulls**	49	76	.392
4=	**New Jersey Nets**	16	25	.390
=	**Houston Rockets**	39	61	.390
=	**San Antonio Spurs**	39	61	.390
7	**Philadelphia 76ers**	74	122	.378
8	**Milwaukee Bucks**	37	63	.370
9	**New York Knicks**	60	117	.339
10	**Phoenix Suns**	35	69	.337

Winning on the road is difficult. Home-team fans distract visiting teams with deafening cheers, foam fingers, and handmade signs. The Lakers' ability to win on the road during the playoffs reflects the team's focus in some of the league's most hostile environments.

DID YOU KNOW?

Even though the Baltimore Bullets won an NBA title in the league's second season, the team eventually disbanded after eight seasons in the NBA.

THE TOP 10

All-Time Home Records

	TEAM	W	L	PCT
1=	Cleveland Rebels*	1	0	1.000
=	Sheboygan Redskins*	1	0	1.000
3	Baltimore Bullets*	7	1	.875
4	Chicago Bulls	98	30	.766
5	Anderson Packers*	3	1	.750
6	Los Angeles Lakers	236	82	.742
7	Boston Celtics	190	70	.731
8	Utah Jazz	70	30	.700
9	Portland Trail Blazers	67	30	.691
10	Indiana Pacers	42	19	.689

The Cleveland Rebels may have lasted only one season but they own the distinction of being No. 1 on the NBA's All-Time Home Records Playoffs chart. The Rebels won their lone home playoff game during the NBA's inaugural season, defeating the New York Knicks, 77-51, on April 2, 1947, in their very first postseason game.

STAMPEDING TO GREATNESS

What did the Chicago Bulls do for an encore after the team won its first-ever NBA championship in 1991? They followed up the next season with an even more impressive run, stampeding to a 67-15 record en route to the franchise's second NBA championship. The Bulls defeated the Portland Trail Blazers in six games in the 1992 NBA Finals, as Michael Jordan picked up his second consecutive NBA Finals MVP trophy.

THE NBA'S GREATEST DYNASTY

The Boston Celtics set a standard of excellence in the NBA that has never been matched. One of three charter franchises when the Basketball Association of America was formed in 1946, the team won its first NBA championship title 11 years later in 1957, and currently flies more title banners from the FleetCenter's rafters than any other franchise.

"Once we won the first time, we were so certain that nobody would beat us," said Bob Cousy, the Celtics' Hall-of-Fame point guard.

Two years later, Cousy certainly proved correct: The Celtics went on a championship run that is unrivaled in all of sports. Boston won an unprecedented eight NBA championships in a row and 11 in 13 seasons. The Celtics' run from 1956 to 1969 included a regular-season record of 716-299 (.705) and a postseason mark of 108-59 (.647). No other franchise in any other professional sport—baseball's New York Yankees, hockey's Montreal Canadiens, or football's Green Bay Packers—can match "The Celtics Tradition" of winning.

BANK SHOT

THE TOP 10

All-Time Playoff Winningest Coaches

	COACH	W	L	PCT
1	Phil Jackson	162	60	.730
2	Pat Riley	155	100	.608
3	Red Auerbach*	99	69	.589
4	K. C. Jones*	81	57	.587
5	Lenny Wilkens	80	94	.460
6	Jerry Sloan	78	80	.494
7	Chuck Daly*	75	51	.595
8=	Larry Brown	69	72	.489
=	Don Nelson	69	81	.460
10	Billy Cunningham*	66	39	.629

PLAYERS' COACH

When Chuck Daly took over as head coach of the Detroit Pistons in 1983, the team had never enjoyed back-to-back winning seasons. All of that changed as Daly instituted a defensive approach to the game. The Pistons went on to win three Central Division titles and back-to-back NBA championships.

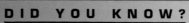

DID YOU KNOW?
Chuck Daly led the 1992 US Men's Olympic Team—The Dream Team—to a gold medal.

THE TOP 10

All-Time Playoff Coaches Ranked by Games

COACH	GAMES
1 Pat Riley	255
2 Phil Jackson	222
3 Lenny Wilkens	174
4 Red Auerbach*	168
5 Jerry Sloan	158
6 Don Nelson	150
7 Larry Brown	141
8 K. C. Jones*	138
9 =Chuck Daly*	126
=George Karl*	126

Leading a team to the NBA Playoffs year after year is a sign of great success and who better to illustrate that than Pat Riley. The three-time NBA Coach of the Year has maintained a standard of excellence with three different franchises—the Los Angeles Lakers, New York Knicks, and Miami Heat—over the course of two-plus decades.

RINGS OF HONOR

Pat Riley proudly displays his six NBA championship rings. The former Miami Heat coach won four as the head coach of the L.A. Lakers during the 1980s, and one as an assistant. Riley also earned a ring playing for the 1971–72 Lakers.

THE TOP 10

All-Time Playoff Coaches Ranked by Winning Percentage†

COACH	PCT	W	L
1 Phil Jackson	.730	162	60
2 Butch Van Breda Kolff*	.636	21	12
3 John Kundla*	.632	60	35
4 Billy Cunningham*	.629	66	39
5 Byron Scott	.625	25	15
6 Larry Costello*	.617	37	23
7 Larry Bird*	.615	32	20
8 Gregg Popovich	.610	47	30
9 Pat Riley	.608	155	100
10 Chuck Daly*	.595	75	51

† 25 games minimum

THE CHAMPIONSHIP TOUCH

Phil Jackson arrived in Los Angeles in 1999 with one goal in mind: lead the Lakers back to NBA championship glory. The franchise featured two All-Stars in Shaquille O'Neal and Kobe Bryant yet struggled to find the right championship mix in the playoffs. The former coach of the Chicago Bulls—who led them to six titles in eight seasons—knew how to maximize his talent. The players bought into Jackson's team-first philosophy, featuring the triangle offense, and stormed to a 67-15 record, the second best in franchise history.

The Lakers not only marched to the NBA championship that season but managed to win two more titles as well, placing them among the NBA's elite. Only the Minneapolis Lakers, Boston Celtics, and Chicago Bulls—the other NBA dynasties—managed to win three or more titles in a row. The coaching success of Jackson has placed him among the all-time coaching greats in NBA history. The 1995–96 NBA Coach of the Year is tied with the legendary Red Auerbach for most NBA titles with nine, and he was named one of the Top 10 Coaches in NBA History in 1996.

TEAM BY TEAM

Team Records 64
Team Leaders 72

SEVENTH HEAVEN

*The 1964–65 Boston Celtics continued the tradition of
championship excellence as the franchise won its seventh
consecutive title. Featuring Bill Russell, Sam Jones, K. C. Jones,
and John Havlicek, the '64–65 Celtics were voted as one of the
Top 10 Teams in NBA History in 1996.*

FLYING HIGH

Steve Smith made an impact during his four-and-a-half season stay in Atlanta. Smith ranks second in franchise history in three-point field goals made and attempted as well as average minutes played per game for a season with 37.3. Smith also boasts the eighth highest single-season scoring average with 18.6.

THE TOP 10

Atlanta Hawks
Last 10 Seasons

SEASON	RECORD	FINISH
2002–2003	35-47	5th/C.Division
2001–2002	33-49	6th/C.Division
2000–2001	25-57	7th/C.Division
1999–2000	28-54	7th/C.Division
1998–1999	31-19	2nd/C.Division
1997–1998	50-32	4th/C.Division
1996–1997	56-26	2nd/C.Division
1995–1996	46-36	T 4th/C.Division
1994–1995	42-40	5th/C.Division
1993–1994	57-25	1st/C.Division

The Blackhawks originated in the Tri-Cities area in 1949. After moving to Milwaukee in 1951, they renamed themselves the Hawks. Four seasons later, the Hawks flew south to St. Louis, where they won an NBA title in 1958. They landed in Atlanta in 1968.

THE TOP 10

Chicago Bulls
Last 10 Seasons

SEASON	RECORD	FINISH
2002–2003	30-52	6th/C.Division
2001–2002	21-61	8th/C.Division
2000–2001	15-67	8th/C.Division
1999–2000	17-65	8th/C.Division
1998–1999	13-37	8th/C.Division
1997–1998	62-20	1st/C.Division
1996–1997	69-13	1st/C.Division
1995–1996	72-10	1st/C.Division
1994–1995	47-35	3rd/C.Division
1993–1994	55-27	2nd/C.Division

The Chicago Bulls began play in 1966, and made the playoffs in their inaugural season. Twenty-five years later, the franchise won its first ever NBA championship. The 1991 title sparked one of the greatest championship runs in NBA history, as the Bulls won six titles in eight seasons. Only the Boston Celtics have won more in that timespan.

THE TOP 10

Boston Celtics
Last 10 Seasons

SEASON	RECORD	FINISH
2002–2003	44-38	3rd/A.Division
2001–2002	49-33	2nd/A.Division
2000–2001	36-46	5th/A.Division
1999–2000	35-47	5th/A.Division
1998–1999	19-31	5th/A.Division
1997–1998	36-46	6th/A.Division
1996–1997	15-67	7th/A.Division
1995–1996	33-49	5th/A.Division
1994–1995	35-47	3rd/A.Division
1993–1994	32-50	5th/A.Division

The NBA's most successful franchise, the Boston Celtics boast 16 championships. The Celtics played their first game in the Basketball Association of America, the forerunner to the NBA, on November 5, 1946, and are one of the three charter members of the NBA. The Celtics Green and the winking leprechaun have symbolized excellence since the team's start.

THE TOP 10

Cleveland Cavaliers
Last 10 Seasons

SEASON	RECORD	FINISH
2002–2003	17-65	8th/C.Division
2001–2002	29-53	7th/C.Division
2000–2001	30-52	6th/C.Division
1999–2000	32-50	6th/C.Division
1998–1999	22-28	7th/C.Division
1997–1998	47-35	5th/C.Division
1996–1997	43-39	4th/C.Division
1995–1996	47-35	5th/C.Division
1994–1995	43-49	4th/C.Division
1993–1994	47-35	T 3rd/C.Division

The Cavaliers began play in 1970, and made their first playoff appearance in 1976, when they lost the Eastern Conference Finals to the Celtics. The Cavaliers made it once more to the conference finals when they lost to the Bulls in 1992.

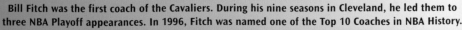
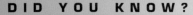

DID YOU KNOW?

Bill Fitch was the first coach of the Cavaliers. During his nine seasons in Cleveland, he led them to three NBA Playoff appearances. In 1996, Fitch was named one of the Top 10 Coaches in NBA History.

THE TOP 10

Dallas Mavericks Last 10 Seasons

SEASON	RECORD	FINISH
2002–2003	60-22	2nd/M.Division
2001–2002	57-25	2nd/M.Division
2000–2001	53-29	T 2nd/M.Division
1999–2000	40-42	4th/M.Division
1998–1999	19-31	5th/M.Division
1997–1998	20-62	5th/M.Division
1996–1997	24-58	4th/M.Division
1995–1996	26-56	T 5th/M.Division
1994–1995	36-46	5th/M.Division
1993–1994	13-69	6th/M.Division

MOTOR CITY REVIVAL

For nine seasons, the Pistons called Fort Wayne, Indiana, home. The team then moved to Detroit in 1957, and have since won two NBA titles (1989 and '90). Richard Hamilton (above) and the Pistons are hoping to motor the franchise to its third NBA title.

THE TOP 10

Detroit Pistons Last 10 Seasons

SEASON	RECORD	FINISH
2002–2003	50-32	1st/C.Division
2001–2002	50-32	1st/C.Division
2000–2001	32-50	5th/C.Division
1999–2000	42-40	T 4th/C.Division
1998–1999	29-21	3rd/C.Division
1997–1998	37-45	6th/C.Division
1996–1997	54-28	T 3rd/C.Division
1995–1996	46-36	T 4th/C.Division
1994–1995	28-54	7th/C.Division
1993–1994	20-62	T 6th/C.Division

A DALLAS COMEBACK

After making the postseason six times in the team's first 10 years, the Mavs experienced a 10-season playoff drought. Their luck changed with the arrival of players such as Steve Nash (left) and Dirk Nowitzki. Now the Mavericks are NBA championship contenders.

THE TOP 10

Denver Nuggets Last 10 Seasons

SEASON	RECORD	FINISH
2002–2003	17-65	7th/M.Division
2001–2002	27-55	6th/M.Division
2000–2001	40-42	6th/M.Division
1999–2000	35-47	5th/M.Division
1998–1999	14-36	6th/M.Division
1997–1998	11-71	7th/M.Division
1996–1997	21-61	5th/M.Division
1995–1996	35-47	4th/M.Division
1994–1995	41-41	4th/M.Division
1993–1994	42-40	4th/M.Division

The Nuggets can be traced to the American Basketball Association, where they spent seven seasons. The franchise has featured some of the game's best players—David Thompson, Dan Issel, Alex English, and Kiki Vandeweghe—and have provided some of the greatest scoring teams.

THE TOP 10

Golden State Warriors Last 10 Seasons

SEASON	RECORD	FINISH
2002–2003	38-44	6th/P.Division
2001–2002	21-61	7th/P.Division
2000–2001	17-65	7th/P.Division
1999–2000	19-63	6th/P.Division
1998–1999	21-29	6th/P.Division
1997–1998	19-63	6th/P.Division
1996–1997	30-52	7th/P.Division
1995–1996	36-46	6th/P.Division
1994–1995	26-56	6th/P.Division
1993–1994	50-32	3rd/P.Division

Six of the 50 Greatest Players have spent at least part of their careers with the Warriors (who moved from Philadelphia to the West Coast in 1962): Paul Arizin, Rick Barry, Wilt Chamberlain, Jerry Lucas, Nate Thurmond, and Robert Parish.

TEAM RECORDS

HAKEEM THE DREAM

Hakeem Olajuwon spent 17 seasons in Houston, where he led the Rockets to 14 NBA Playoff appearances. In 1996, Olajuwon was named as one of the 50 Greatest Players in NBA History.

THE TOP 10

Houston Rockets Last 10 Seasons

SEASON	RECORD	FINISH
2002–2003	43-39	5th/M.Division
2001–2002	28-54	5th/M.Division
2000–2001	45-37	5th/M.Division
1999–2000	34-48	6th/M.Division
1998–1999	31-19	3rd/M.Division
1997–1998	41-41	4th/M.Division
1996–1997	57-25	2nd/M.Division
1995–1996	48-34	3rd/M.Division
1994–1995	47-35	3rd/M.Division
1993–1994	58-24	1st/M.Division

THE TOP 10

Los Angeles Clippers Last 10 Seasons

SEASON	RECORD	FINISH
2002–2003	27-55	7th/P.Division
2001–2002	39-43	5th/P.Division
2000–2001	31-51	6th/P.Division
1999–2000	15-67	7th/P.Division
1998–1999	9-41	7th/P.Division
1997–1998	17-65	7th/P.Division
1996–1997	36-46	5th/P.Division
1995–1996	29-53	7th/P.Division
1994–1995	17-65	7th/P.Division
1993–1994	27-55	7th/P.Division

Originating in Buffalo, New York, in 1970, as the Braves, the franchise moved to San Diego in 1978, and became the Clippers. The team moved to its current home, Los Angeles, in 1984.

THE TOP 10

Indiana Pacers Last 10 Seasons

SEASON	RECORD	FINISH
2002–2003	48-34	2nd/C.Division
2001–2002	42-40	T 3rd/C.Division
2000–2001	41-41	4th/C.Division
1999–2000	56-26	1st/C.Division
1998–1999	33-17	1st/C.Division
1997–1998	58-24	2nd/C.Division
1996–1997	39-43	6th/C.Division
1995–1996	52-30	2nd/C.Division
1994–1995	52-30	1st/C.Division
1993–1994	47-35	T 3rd/C.Division

One of four former American Basketball Association franchises that joined the NBA in 1976, the Pacers have won the Central Division title three times in the last 10 seasons. The Pacers even advanced to the NBA Finals in 2000.

THE TOP 10

Los Angeles Lakers Last 10 Seasons

SEASON	RECORD	FINISH
2002–2003	50-32	2nd/P.Division
2001–2002	58-24	2nd/P.Division
2000–2001	56-26	1st/P.Division
1999–2000	67-15	1st/P.Division
1998–1999	31-19	2nd/P.Division
1997–1998	61-21	T 1st/P.Division
1996–1997	56-26	2nd/P.Division
1995–1996	53-29	2nd/P.Division
1994–1995	48-34	3rd/P.Division
1993–1994	39-43	5th/P.Division

Only one other team, the Boston Celtics, have won more championships (16) than the Lakers and their 14 banners. The franchise called Minneapolis home before moving to L.A. in 1960.

THE TOP 10

Memphis Grizzlies
Last 8 Seasons

SEASON	RECORD	FINISH
2002–2003	28-54	6th/M.Division
2001–2002	23-59	7th/M.Division
2000–2001	23-59	7th/M.Division
1999–2000	22-60	7th/M.Division
1998–1999	8-42	7th/M.Division
1997–1998	19-63	6th/M.Division
1996–1997	14-68	7th/M.Division
1995–1996	15-67	7th/M.Division

When the Grizzlies entered the NBA in 1995, they were located in Vancouver, British Columbia. The team moved to Memphis, Tennessee, in 2001.

THE TOP 10

Miami Heat
Last 10 Seasons

SEASON	RECORD	FINISH
2002–2003	25-57	7th/A.Division
2001–2002	36-46	6th/A.Division
2000–2001	50-32	2nd/A.Division
1999–2000	52-30	1st/A.Division
1998–1999	33-17	T 1st/A.Division
1997–1998	55-27	1st/A.Division
1996–1997	61-21	1st/A.Division
1995–1996	42-40	3rd/A.Division
1994–1995	32-50	4th/A.Division
1993–1994	42-40	4th/A.Division

KUKOC AND THE BUCKS

The Milwaukee Bucks entered the NBA in 1968 and won the NBA championship in only its third season, sweeping the Baltimore Bullets. Now Toni Kukoc is trying to lead the team to playoff glory.

THE TOP 10

Milwaukee Bucks
Last 10 Seasons

SEASON	RECORD	FINISH
2002–2003	42-40	4th/C.Division
2001–2002	41-41	5th/C.Division
2000–2001	52-30	1st/C.Division
1999–2000	42-40	T 4th/C.Division
1998–1999	28-22	4th/C.Division
1997–1998	36-46	4th/C.Division
1996–1997	33-49	7th/C.Division
1995–1996	25-57	7th/C.Division
1994–1995	34-48	7th/C.Division
1993–1994	20-62	T 6th/C.Division

RISING HEAT

Tim Hardaway enjoyed great success in leading the Miami Heat. The 6-0 point guard helped the Heat secure four Atlantic Division championships during his five-plus seasons in Miami, including an Eastern Conference Finals appearance in 1997.

NBA.COM FUN FACT

Tim Hardaway is the Miami Heat's all-time assists leader with 2,867 (1995–96 through 2000–01).

67

Minnesota Timberwolves Last 10 Seasons

SEASON	RECORD	FINISH
2002–2003	51-31	3rd/M.Division
2001–2002	50-32	3rd/M.Division
2000–2001	47-35	4th/M.Division
1999–2000	50-32	3rd/M.Division
1998–1999	25-25	4th/M.Division
1997–1998	45-37	3rd/M.Division
1996–1997	40-42	3rd/M.Division
1995–1996	26-56	T 5th/M.Division
1994–1995	21-61	6th/M.Division
1993–1994	20-62	5th/M.Division

The Minnesota Timberwolves entered the NBA prior to the 1989–90 season, joining the Orlando Magic as the NBA's newest expansion teams.

New Orleans Hornets Last 10 Seasons

SEASON	RECORD	FINISH
2002–2003	47-35	3rd/C.Division
2001–2002	44-38	2nd/C.Division
2000–2001	46-36	3rd/C.Division
1999–2000	49-33	2nd/C.Division
1998–1999	26-24	5th/C.Division
1997–1998	51-31	3rd/C.Division
1996–1997	54-28	T 3rd/C.Division
1995–1996	41-41	6th/C.Division
1994–1995	50-32	2nd/C.Division
1993–1994	41-41	5th/C.Division

New Orleans welcomed its second NBA team when the Hornets arrived for the 2002–03 season. The city was home to the Jazz for five seasons (1974–75 to 1978–79) and featured one of the game's greatest players, "Pistol" Pete Maravich.

New Jersey Nets Last 10 Seasons

SEASON	RECORD	FINISH
2002–2003	49-33	1st/A.Division
2001–2002	52-30	1st/A.Division
2000–2001	26-56	6th/A.Division
1999–2000	31-51	6th/A.Division
1998–1999	16-34	7th/A.Division
1997–1998	43-49	T 2nd/A.Division
1996–1997	26-56	5th/A.Division
1995–1996	30-52	6th/A.Division
1994–1995	30-52	5th/A.Division
1993–1994	45-37	3rd/A.Division

The Nets were one of four ABA teams to join the NBA prior to the 1976–77 season. Despite winning two championships in the ABA, the Nets advanced beyond the NBA Playoffs first round only once in 11 appearances. Jason Kidd's arrival for the 2001–02 season changed everything. He led the team to the NBA Finals in 2002 and 2003.

INSTANT IMPACT

In the 10 seasons before Ewing's arrival in 1985, the Knicks made the playoffs four times. During Ewing's 15 seasons in New York, the Knicks reached the postseason 13 times. Ewing's team records include points (23,665), rebounds (10,759), and blocks (2,758).

New York Knicks Last 10 Seasons

SEASON	RECORD	FINISH
2002–2003	37-45	6th/A.Division
2001–2002	30-52	7th/A.Division
2000–2001	48-34	3rd/A.Division
1999–2000	50-32	2nd/A.Division
1998–1999	27-23	4th/A.Division
1997–1998	43-39	T 2nd/A.Division
1996–1997	57-25	2nd/A.Division
1995–1996	47-35	2nd/A.Division
1994–1995	55-27	2nd/A.Division
1993–1994	57-25	1st/A.Division

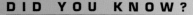

DID YOU KNOW?
Patrick Ewing (33) was the eighth Knick to have his number retired, joining Walt Frazier (10), Dick Barnett (12), Earl Monroe (15), Dick McGuire (15), Willis Reed (19), Dave DeBusschere (22), and Bill Bradley (24).

THE TOP 10

Orlando Magic
Last 10 Seasons

SEASON	RECORD	FINISH
2002–2003	42-40	4th/A.Division
2001–2002	44-38	3rd/A.Division
2000–2001	43-39	4th/A.Division
1999–2000	41-41	4th/A.Division
1998–1999	33-17	1st/A.Division
1997–1998	41-41	5th/A.Division
1996–1997	45-37	3rd/A.Division
1995–1996	60-22	1st/A.Division
1994–1995	57-25	1st/A.Division
1993–1994	50-32	2nd/A.Division

A MAGICAL ARRIVAL

The arrival of Penny Hardaway created basketball Magic for Orlando fans. He earned NBA All-Rookie First Team honors and teamed with Shaquille O'Neal to form one of the best tandems in the NBA. The Magic won their division title in back-to-back seasons.

THE TOP 10

Philadelphia 76ers
Last 10 Seasons

SEASON	RECORD	FINISH
2002–2003	48-34	2nd/A.Division
2001–2002	43-39	4th/A.Division
2000–2001	56-26	1st/A.Division
1999–2000	49-33	3rd/A.Division
1998–1999	28-22	3rd/A.Division
1997–1998	31-51	7th/A.Division
1996–1997	22-60	6th/A.Division
1995–1996	18-64	7th/A.Division
1994–1995	24-58	6th/A.Division
1993–1994	25-57	6th/A.Division

In the spring of 1963, the Syracuse Nationals were sold to Philadelphia businessmen Irv Kosloff and Ike Richman, and the Philadelphia 76ers began play in the NBA in the 1963–64 season. Since then, the franchise has made six NBA Finals appearances and netted two NBA championships.

THE TOP 10

Phoenix Suns
Last 10 Seasons

SEASON	RECORD	FINISH
2002–2003	44-38	4th/P.Division
2001–2002	36-46	6th/P.Division
2000–2001	51-31	3rd/P.Division
1999–2000	53-29	3rd/P.Division
1998–1999	27-23	T 3rd/P.Division
1997–1998	56-26	3rd/P.Division
1996–1997	40-42	4th/P.Division
1995–1996	41-41	4th/P.Division
1994–1995	59-23	1st/P.Division
1993–1994	56-26	2nd/P.Division

THUNDER DAN

Dan Majerle enjoyed great success in Phoenix, helping lead the Suns to the 1993 NBA Finals. Majerle played six seasons in the Valley of the Sun before moving on to Cleveland and Miami. He returned to Phoenix for the 2002–03 season before retiring.

TEAM RECORDS

Portland Trail Blazers Last 10 Seasons

SEASON	RECORD	FINISH
2002–2003	50-32	3rd/P.Division
2001–2002	49-33	3rd/P.Division
2000–2001	50-32	4th/P.Division
1999–2000	59-23	2nd/P.Division
1998–1999	35-15	1st/P.Division
1997–1998	46-36	4th/P.Division
1996–1997	49-33	3rd/P.Division
1995–1996	44-38	3rd/P.Division
1994–1995	44-38	4th/P.Division
1993–1994	47-35	4th/P.Division

Sacramento Kings Last 10 Seasons

SEASON	RECORD	FINISH
2002–2003	59-23	1st/P.Division
2001–2002	61-21	1st/P.Division
2000–2001	55-27	2nd/P.Division
1999–2000	44-38	5th/P.Division
1998–1999	27-23	T 3rd/P.Division
1997–1998	27-55	5th/P.Division
1996–1997	34-48	6th/P.Division
1995–1996	39-43	5th/P.Division
1994–1995	39-43	5th/P.Division
1993–1994	28-54	6th/P.Division

San Antonio Spurs Last 10 Seasons

SEASON	RECORD	FINISH
2002–2003	60-22	1st/M.Division
2001–2002	58-24	1st/M.Division
2000–2001	58-24	1st/M.Division
1999–2000	53-29	2nd/M.Division
1998–1999	37-13	T 1st/M.Division
1997–1998	56-26	2nd/M.Division
1996–1997	20-62	6th/M.Division
1995–1996	59-23	1st/M.Division
1994–1995	62-20	1st/M.Division
1993–1994	55-27	2nd/M.Division

SPURS OF THE MOMENT

The San Antonio Spurs celebrated the 2003 NBA championship after defeating the New Jersey Nets. It was the Spurs' second NBA title in five years. The team first won in 1999.

THE TOP 10

Seattle SuperSonics Last 10 Seasons

SEASON	RECORD	FINISH
2002–2003	40-42	5th/P.Division
2001–2002	45-37	4th/P.Division
2000–2001	44-38	5th/P.Division
1999–2000	45-37	4th/P.Division
1998–1999	25-25	5th/P.Division
1997–1998	61-21	T 1st/P.Division
1996–1997	57-25	1st/P.Division
1995–1996	64-18	1st/P.Division
1994–1995	57-25	2nd/P.Division
1993–1994	63-19	1st/P.Division

UTAH JAZZ LEGENDS
Karl Malone and John Stockton not only played for the Jazz for 18 seasons together, but were also teammates on the 1992 and 1996 Dream Teams that won Olympic gold medals in Barcelona and Atlanta, respectively.

SEATTLE'S SUPERSONIC
The Seattle SuperSonics have made three NBA Finals appearances in their history, netting one championship in 1978. Detlef Schrempf helped lead the Sonics to the 1996 NBA Finals versus the Chicago Bulls, who won the title in six games.

Utah Jazz Last 10 Seasons

SEASON	RECORD	FINISH
2002–2003	47-35	4th/M.Division
2001–2002	44-38	4th/M.Division
2000–2001	53-29	T 2nd/M.Division
1999–2000	55-27	1st/M.Division
1998–1999	37-13	T 1st/M.Division
1997–1998	62-20	1st/M.Division
1996–1997	64-18	1st/M.Division
1995–1996	55-27	2nd/M.Division
1994–1995	60-22	2nd/M.Division
1993–1994	53-29	3rd/M.Division

Stockton and Malone were a model of consistency and greatness for the Utah Jazz. They led their team to the playoffs every season, including two NBA Finals' appearances in 1997 and '98.

Toronto Raptors Last 8 Seasons

SEASON	RECORD	FINISH
2002–2003	24-58	7th/C.Division
2001–2002	42-40	T 3rd/C.Division
2000–2001	47-35	2nd/C.Division
1999–2000	45-37	3rd/C.Division
1998–1999	23-27	6th/C.Division
1997–1998	16-66	8th/C.Division
1996–1997	30-52	8th/C.Division
1995–1996	21-61	8th/C.Division

The Toronto Raptors entered the NBA in 1995, marking the second time the city has been home to an NBA franchise. The Toronto Huskies were a member of the Basketball Association of America, the forerunner to the NBA, and played in the league's very first game on November 1, 1946. The Huskies folded after only one season.

Washington Wizards Last 10 Seasons

SEASON	RECORD	FINISH
2002–2003	37-45	5th/A.Division
2001–2002	37-45	5th/A.Division
2000–2001	19-63	7th/A.Division
1999–2000	29-53	7th/A.Division
1998–1999	18-32	6th/A.Division
1997–1998	42-40	4th/A.Division
1996–1997	44-38	4th/A.Division
1995–1996	39-43	4th/A.Division
1994–1995	21-61	7th/A.Division
1993–1994	24-58	7th/A.Division

Starting in Chicago in 1961 as the Packers, they were renamed the Zephyrs before arriving in Baltimore in 1963, when they were known as the Bullets and then the Capital Bullets after moving to Landover, Maryland. The team became the Washington Bullets in 1974, and finally the Wizards in 1997, after moving to Washington, DC.

TEAM LEADERS

Atlanta Hawks

	PLAYER	POINTS
1	Dominique Wilkins*	23,292
2	Bob Pettit*	20,880
3	Lou Hudson*	16,049
4	Cliff Hagan*	13,447
5	John Drew*	12,621
6	Kevin Willis	10,495
7	Eddie Johnson*	9,631
8	Zelmo Beaty*	8,727
9	Bill Bridges*	8,685
10	Lenny Wilkens*	8,591

Only three players in the Atlanta Hawks' history have received the honor of having their respective jerseys retired: Dominique Wilkins, Bob Pettit, and Lou Hudson. Those three players also happen to rank as the top three scorers in the team's 50-plus-year history. The all-time leader, Wilkins, scored 23,292 points in 11 and a half seasons, while Pettit scored 20,880 points in 11 seasons. Hudson scored his 16,049 points in nine.

Boston Celtics

	PLAYER	POINTS
1	John Havlicek*	26,395
2	Larry Bird*	21,791
3	Robert Parish*	18,245
4	Kevin McHale*	17,335
5	Bob Cousy*	16,955
6	Sam Jones*	15,411
7	Bill Russell*	14,522
8	Dave Cowens*	13,192
9	Jo Jo White*	13,188
10	Bill Sharman*	12,287

A BOSTON GREAT

John Havlicek is considered one of the greatest all-around players in NBA history. The 13-time NBA All-Star helped lead the Boston Celtics to eight NBA championships in 16 seasons. The Celtics' all-time leading scorer averaged 20.8 points per game.

Chicago Bulls

	PLAYER	POINTS
1	Michael Jordan*	29,277
2	Scottie Pippen	14,987
3	Bob Love*	12,623
4	Jerry Sloan*	10,233
5	Chet Walker*	9,788
6	Artis Gilmore*	9,288
7	Reggie Theus*	8,279
8	Horace Grant	6,866
9	Norm Van Lier*	6,505
10	Toni Kukoc	6,148

Michael Jordan and Scottie Pippen weren't the only great Chicago Bulls to put on the red, white, and black uniform. Jerry Sloan and Bob Love starred for Chicago in the late 1960s and '70s. Sloan earned the reputation as one of the NBA's toughest defenders while Love led the Bulls in scoring for seven straight seasons. Both players have their numbers hanging in the rafters.

JAZZ LEADER

He is one of the most successful coaches in NBA history. For more than a decade, Jerry Sloan has guided the Utah Jazz to 14 consecutive NBA Playoff series, five Midwest Division titles, and back-to-back NBA Finals appearances in 1997 and '98. The impressive résumé doesn't end there. Sloan is only the third coach in NBA history to win at least 50 games in 10 seasons, joining Pat Riley and Phil Jackson, and ranks in the top 10 in all-time coaching victories. The same characteristics that propelled him to star status in the NBA—hard work, unparalleled work ethic—have been applied to his career as a head coach.

Sloan earned the nickname "The Original Bull" after the Chicago Bulls picked him with their first selection in the 1966 NBA Expansion Draft. Sloan became a four-time NBA All-Defensive First Team selection and is one of only 18 players in NBA history ever to be voted to the league's All-Defensive First Team at least four times. He retired following the 1975–76 season to become the Bulls' assistant coach for two seasons before becoming the team's head coach for three seasons. Sloan later served as an assistant coach for the Jazz for four years before taking over in 1988.

The Top 10 Cleveland Cavaliers

Player/Points

1 Brad Daugherty* 10,389 **2** Austin Carr* 10,265 **3** Mark Price* 9,543 **4** Bingo Smith* 9,513 **5** John Williams* 8,504 **6** Larry Nance* 7,257 **7** Campy Russell* 6,588 **8** World B. Free* 6,329 **9** Terrell Brandon 5,793 **10** Jim Chones* 5,729

THE TOP 10
Dallas Mavericks

	PLAYER	POINTS
1	Rolando Blackman*	16,643
2	Mark Aguirre*	13,930
3	Derek Harper*	12,597
4	Michael Finley	10,044
5	Brad Davis*	7,623
6	Dirk Nowitzki	7,394
7	Sam Perkins*	6,766
8	Jay Vincent*	6,464
9	Jim Jackson	5,660
10	Steve Nash	4,809

The first overall selection of the 1981 NBA Draft, Mark Aguirre was an instant star for the Dallas Mavericks. Aguirre averaged 18.7 points during his rookie season and 29.5 in only his third.

THE TOP 10
Detroit Pistons

	PLAYER	POINTS
1	Isiah Thomas*	18,822
2	Joe Dumars*	16,401
3	Bob Lanier*	15,488
4	David Bing*	15,235
5	Bill Laimbeer*	12,665
6	Vinnie Johnson*	10,146
7	Grant Hill	9,393
8	John Long*	9,023
9	Bailey Howell*	8,182
10	Gene Shue*	8,034

Few had heard of Joe Dumars when he entered the NBA in 1985. Fourteen years, 16,401 points, one NBA Finals MVP, and two championship rings later, Joe D. is a household name.

THE TOP 10
Denver Nuggets

	PLAYER	POINTS
1	Alex English*	21,645
2	Dan Issel*	14,659
3	David Thompson*	9,834
4	Fat Lever*	8,081
5	Mahmoud Abdul-Rauf*	7,029
6	Kiki Vandeweghe*	6,829
7	Antonio McDyess	6,555
8	Reggie Williams*	5,934
9	Michael Adams*	5,534
10	LaPhonso Ellis*	5,201

THE TOP 10
Golden State Warriors

	PLAYER	POINTS
1	Wilt Chamberlain*	17,783
2	Rick Barry*	16,447
3	Paul Arizin*	16,266
4	Chris Mullin*	16,235
5	Nate Thurmond*	13,191
6	Jeff Mullins*	12,547
7	Purvis Short*	11,894
8	Neil Johnston*	10,023
9	Joe Barry Carroll*	9,996
10	Tim Hardaway	8,337

RECORD-SETTER

Who set 31 Denver Nuggets records in 10 seasons, including points scored (21,645), games played (837), assists (3,679), and scoring average (25.9 ppg)? The answer: Alex English.

TEAM LEADERS

THE TOP 10
Houston Rockets

	PLAYER	POINTS
1	Hakeem Olajuwon*	26,511
2	Calvin Murphy*	17,949
3	Rudy Tomjanovich*	13,383
4	Elvin Hayes*	11,762
5	Moses Malone*	11,119
6	Robert Reid*	8,823
7	Mike Newlin*	8,480
8	Otis Thorpe*	8,177
9	Allen Leavell*	6,684
10	Cuttino Mobley	6,188

The first overall pick of the 1968 NBA Draft, Elvin Hayes showed why he was the Houston Rockets' top selection. As a rookie, the 6-9 forward led the NBA in scoring (28.4) and minutes (3,695) and was named to the NBA All-Rookie Team.

THE TOP 10
Indiana Pacers

	PLAYER	POINTS
1	Reggie Miller	23,505
2	Rik Smits*	12,871
3	Vern Fleming*	9,535
4	Chuck Person*	9,096
5	Herb Williams*	8,637
6	Billy Knight*	7,440
7	Dale Davis	6,081
8	Detlef Schrempf*	6,009
9	Jalen Rose	5,712
10	Steve Stipanovich*	5,323

Not only is Reggie Miller the Indiana Pacers' all-time leading scorer but he's also the franchise leader in steals as well. The 11th overall pick of the 1987 NBA Draft, Miller has remained with the Pacers throughout his All-Star career.

THE TOP 10
Los Angeles Clippers

	PLAYER	POINTS
1	Randy Smith*	12,735
2	Bob McAdoo*	9,434
3	Danny Manning*	7,120
4	Loy Vaught*	6,614
5	Ken Norman*	6,432
6	Ron Harper*	5,853
7	Benoit Benjamin*	5,405
8	Eric Piatkowski	5,269
9	Charles Smith*	4,994
10	Bob Kauffman*	4,847

Bob McAdoo starred for the Buffalo Braves in the 1970s. In four seasons, McAdoo won three scoring titles and one NBA MVP.

THE TOP 10
Los Angeles Lakers

	PLAYER	POINTS
1	Jerry West*	25,192
2	Kareem Abdul-Jabbar*	24,176
3	Elgin Baylor*	23,149
4	Magic Johnson*	17,707
5	James Worthy*	16,320
6	Gail Goodrich*	13,044
7	Byron Scott*	12,780
8	Shaquille O'Neal	12,456
9	George Mikan*	11,351
10	Kobe Bryant	10,658

Jerry West starred for 14 seasons for the Lakers, earning 14 All-Star nods and was a member of the 1972 NBA championship team.

MR. ROCKET

At 5-9, Calvin Murphy may have been undersized but he was able to use his speed and quickness to elude defenders. Murphy spent his entire 13-year career with the Rockets and amassed several team records. He was inducted into the Basketball Hall of Fame in 1993.

THE TOP 10
Memphis Grizzlies

	PLAYER	POINTS
1	Shareef Abdur-Rahim	7,801
2	Bryant Reeves*	4,945
3	Mike Bibby	3,153
4	Pau Gasol	2,996
5	Michael Dickerson	2,710
6	Blue Edwards*	2,393
7	Shane Battier	1,881
8	Jason Williams	1,878
9	Stromile Swift	1,841
10	Greg Anthony*	1,583

The Grizzlies joined the NBA in 1995, and seven years later boasted their first-ever NBA Rookie of the Year. Spanish native Pau Gasol, who was acquired in a 2001 NBA Draft trade from the Atlanta Hawks, averaged 17.6 points and 8.9 rebounds to grab top rookie honors.

THE TOP 10
Milwaukee Bucks

	PLAYER	POINTS
1	Kareem Abdul-Jabbar*	14,211
2	Glenn Robinson	12,010
3	Sidney Moncreif*	11,594
4	Bob Dandridge*	11,478
5	Marques Johnson*	10,980
6	Junior Bridgeman*	9,892
7	Brian Winters*	9,743
8	Ray Allen	9,681
9	Terry Cummings*	9,290
10	Ricky Pierce*	7,570

One of the greatest players to ever put on a Milwaukee Bucks uniform was Sidney Moncrief. The 6-3 guard was a terrific defender who won back-to-back NBA Defensive Player of the Year honors and was named to the league's All-Defensive First Team four times. A four-time NBA All-Star, Moncrief spent 10 seasons in Milwaukee before signing with the Atlanta Hawks in 1990.

THE TOP 10
Miami Heat

	PLAYER	POINTS
1	Glen Rice	9,248
2	Alonzo Mourning	8,045
3	Rony Seikaly*	6,742
4	Tim Hardaway	6,335
5	Grant Long*	5,473
6	Kevin Edwards*	4,362
7	Bimbo Coles	4,003
8	Eddie Jones	3,443
9	Steve Smith	2,882
10	Jamal Mashburn	2,835

THE HEAT IS ON

Glen Rice spent the first six years of his career with the Miami Heat and accumulated several franchise records. In addition to being the Heat's all-time leading scorer, the 6-8 forward also ranks No. 1 in games started, minutes played, consecutive games played, and field goals made and attempted.

NBA.COM FUN FACT
Glen Rice earned NBA All-Star Game MVP honors in 1997 as a member of the Charlotte Hornets. Rice holds the All-Star Game record for most points in a half with 24.

75

WALT "CLYDE" FRAZIER

Walt Frazier averaged 19.3 points during his 10 seasons in New York. The seven-time NBA All-Star was named to seven NBA All-Defensive First Teams and led the Knicks to two NBA championships.

THE TOP 10
New York Knicks

	PLAYER	POINTS
1	Patrick Ewing*	23,665
2	Walt Frazier*	14,617
3	Willis Reed*	12,183
4	Carl Braun*	10,449
5	Richie Guerin*	10,392
6	Allan Houston	10,004
7	Earl Monroe*	9,679
8	Dick Barnett*	9,442
9	Bill Bradley*	9,217
10	Bill Cartwright*	9,006

THE TOP 10
Minnesota Timberwolves

	PLAYER	POINTS
1	Kevin Garnett	11,877
2	Sam Mitchell*	7,161
3	Doug West*	6,216
4	Tony Campbell*	4,888
5	Christian Laettner	4,759
6	Wally Szczerbiak	4,434
7	Isaiah Rider*	4,315
8	Tom Gugliotta	4,201
9	Pooh Richardson*	3,689
10	Anthony Peeler	3,622

Kevin Garnett arrived in Minnesota in 1995, and has been rewriting the franchise's record books ever since. The 2003 NBA All-Star Game MVP is the team leader in points, rebounds, assists, blocked shots, field goals made and attempted.

THE TOP 10
New Jersey Nets

	PLAYER	POINTS
1	Buck Williams*	10,440
2	Derrick Coleman	6,930
3	Chris Morris*	6,762
4	Mike Gminski*	6,415
5	Kerry Kittles	6,024
6	Otis Birdsong*	5,968
7	Keith Van Horn	5,700
8	Albert King*	5,595
9	Kendall Gill	4,932
10	Darwin Cook*	4,699

Derrick Coleman was the second player in franchise history to win the NBA's Rookie of the Year Award. He spent five seasons in New Jersey before being traded to the 76ers in 1995.

MR. NET

Buck Williams won NBA Rookie of the Year honors for the New Jersey Nets in 1981. Williams continued to star for the Nets for seven additional seasons and is the franchise leader in points, rebounds, minutes, field goals made and attempted, and free throws made.

DID YOU KNOW?
Walt Frazier is the New York Knicks' all-time assists leader with 4,791 (1967–68 to 1976–77).

THE TOP 10

New Orleans Hornets

	PLAYER	POINTS
1	Dell Curry*	9,839
2	Larry Johnson*	7,405
3	David Wesley	6,458
4	Glen Rice	5,651
5	Muggsy Bogues*	5,531
6	Alonzo Mourning	4,569
7	Kendall Gill	4,159
8	Jamal Mashburn	4,158
9	Baron Davis	3,957
10	Elden Campbell	3,868

THE TOP 10

Phoenix Suns

	PLAYER	POINTS
1	Walter Davis*	15,666
2	Alvan Adams*	13,910
3	Kevin Johnson*	12,747
4	Dick Van Arsdale*	12,060
5	Paul Westphal*	9,564
6	Larry Nance*	8,430
7	Dan Majerle*	8,034
8	Tom Chambers*	7,817
9	Charles Barkley*	6,556
10	Jeff Hornacek*	6,420

Walter Davis was selected by the Suns with the fifth overall pick in the 1977 NBA Draft and stayed in Phoenix for 11 seasons. Davis won the NBA Rookie of the Year Award after averaging 24.2 points per game. His jersey number 6 was retired in 1994.

ONE-FRANCHISE STAR

Hal Greer played his entire 15-year career with one franchise, starting with the Syracuse Nationals in 1958, and following the team to Philadelphia where they became the 76ers. Greer averaged 19.2 points and 5.0 assists for his career.

THE TOP 10

Orlando Magic

	PLAYER	POINTS
1	Nick Anderson*	10,650
2	Shaquille O'Neal	8,019
3	Anfernee Hardaway	7,018
4	Dennis Scott*	6,603
5	Tracy McGrady	6,420
6	Darrell Armstrong	5,898
7	Scott Skiles*	4,966
8	Horace Grant	4,638
9	Terry Catledge*	3,433
10	Pat Garrity	3,055

Nick Anderson was the first-ever draft pick for the then-expansion franchise, Orlando Magic. The former University of Illinois guard played 10 seasons in Orlando and was a key member of the 1994–95 team that advanced to the NBA Finals.

THE TOP 10

Philadelphia 76ers

	PLAYER	POINTS
1	Hal Greer*	21,586
2	Dolph Schayes*	19,247
3	Julius Erving*	18,364
4	Charles Barkley*	14,184
5	Billy Cunningham*	13,626
6	Allen Iverson	13,170
7	Johnny Kerr*	11,699
8	Maurice Cheeks*	10,429
9	Chet Walker*	9,043
10	Larry Costello*	7,957

After seven NBA seasons, Allen Iverson already ranks sixth (and closing in!) on the Sixers' all-time scoring list. At the start of the 2003–04 season, Iverson was 8,416 points shy of tying Hal Greer's mark of 21,586.

The Top 10 Portland Trail Blazers

Player/Points

① **Clyde Drexler*** 18,040 **②** **Terry Porter*** 11,330 **③** **Clifford Robinson** 10,405
④ **Jerome Kersey*** 10,067 **⑤** **Jim Paxson*** 10,003 **⑥** **Geoff Petrie*** 9,732
⑦ **Mychal Thompson*** 9,215 **⑧** **Sidney Wicks*** 8,882 **⑨** **Rasheed Wallace** 8,353
⑩ **Kevin Duckworth*** 7,188

Clyde Drexler rose to the top of the Trail Blazer scoring charts during his 11-plus seasons in the Rose City. The 6-7 guard is also the franchise leader in rebounds and assists.

THE TOP 10
San Antonio Spurs

PLAYER	POINTS
1 David Robinson*	20,790
2 George Gervin*	19,383
3 Tim Duncan	10,324
4 Mike Mitchell*	9,799
5 Sean Elliott*	9,659
6 Larry Kenon*	6,733
7 Avery Johnson	6,486
8 Alvin Robertson*	6,285
9 Artis Gilmore*	6,127
10 Willie Anderson*	5,946

THE TOP 10
Sacramento Kings

PLAYER	POINTS
1 Oscar Robertson*	22,009
2 Jack Twyman*	15,840
3 Mitch Richmond*	12,070
4 Nate Archibald*	10,894
5 Sam Lacey*	9,895
6 Jerry Lucas*	9,107
7 Eddie Johnson*	9,027
8 Scott Wedman*	9,002
9 Wayne Embry*	8,486
10 Adrian Smith*	8,085

THE BIG O

Oscar Robertson could do it all: pass, rebound, and shoot. For 14 years, "The Big O" showed his versatility and was a devastating offensive force. The 12-time All-Star redefined the point guard position, averaging 25.7 points, 9.5 assists, and 7.5 for his career.

DAVID ROBINSON: COMMUNITY HERO

The list of on-court accomplishments are numerous: NBA Rookie of the Year, NBA MVP, NBA scoring champion, NBA Defensive Player of the Year, two-time NBA champion, and the list goes on and on. Yet as impressive as David Robinson's career has been on the court, it's what he is doing off the court that may define his true legacy.

The 7-1 center, who retired following the 2002–03 season, is devoting his time to his other passion: community service, specifically The Carver Academy. The 10-time NBA All-Star, who is a fixture in the San Antonio community, donated nine million dollars toward the construction and operation of the independent elementary school for students from a culturally diverse community east of downtown San Antonio. The school offers a challenging academic program featuring small classes, leadership opportunities, and a nurturing environment based upon the foundation of Judeo-Christian scripture. Named for George Washington Carver, the school opened on September 17, 2001, with 60 pre-kindergarten through second-grade kids. In June 2003, Carver Academy received, courtesy of the NBA, a Reading and Learning Center (left) equipped with books and computers for the students.

THE TOP 10

Seattle SuperSonics

	PLAYER	POINTS
1	Gary Payton	18,207
2	Fred Brown*	14,018
3	Jack Sikma*	12,034
4	Shawn Kemp	10,148
5	Gus Williams*	9,676
6	Dale Ellis*	9,405
7	Xavier McDaniel*	8,438
8	Spencer Haywood*	8,131
9	Tom Chambers*	8,028
10	Detlef Schrempf*	6,870

"Downtown" Freddie Brown was one of the most popular players ever to put on a Sonics uniform. The sharp-shooting guard was the captain of the 1978–79 Sonics championship team and still holds the franchise's record for most points in a single game with 58. Brown retired in 1984, as the then Sonics' all-time leader in games played, points, field goals, and steals. The only player to wear uniform number 32 in franchise history, the team retired it on November 6, 1986.

THE TOP 10

Toronto Raptors

	PLAYER	POINTS
1	Vince Carter	7,458
2	Doug Christie	4,448
3	Damon Stoudamire	3,917
4	Antonio Davis	3,830
5	Alvin Williams	3,381
6	Morris Peterson	2,783
7	Tracy McGrady	2,122
8	Tracy Murray	1,759
9	Marcus Camby	1,700
10	Charles Oakley	1,644

The Toronto Raptors debuted in 1995–96 and feature Damon Stoudamire, the seventh overall selection of the 1995 NBA Draft. Stoudamire averaged 19 points per game during his first season to pick up NBA Rookie of the Year honors.

THE TOP 10

Utah Jazz

	PLAYER	POINTS
1	Karl Malone	36,374
2	John Stockton*	19,711
3	Adrian Dantley*	13,635
4	Darrell Griffith*	12,391
5	Thurl Bailey*	9,897
6	Pete Maravich*	8,324
7	Rickey Green*	6,917
8	Jeff Hornacek*	6,848
9	Bryon Russell	5,752
10	Mark Eaton*	5,216

The Jazz featured one of the most creative offensive forces in NBA history—"Pistol" Pete Maravich. The 6-5 guard starred for the Jazz for five-plus seasons and was considered one of the game's most spectacular showmen. Between-the-legs passes, behind-the-back passes, unorthodox circus shots, you name it, he would do it. The Hall of Famer notched a 24.2 points-per-game mark in the NBA, which included one scoring title.

THE BIG E

Elvin Hayes's signature move was the turnaround jumper. It was virtually unstoppable and so was his all-around game. The Hall of Famer starred for nine seasons for the Bullets and led the team to three NBA Finals appearances in five years, finally winning the NBA championship in 1978.

THE TOP 10

Washington Wizards

	PLAYER	POINTS
1	Elvin Hayes*	15,551
2	Jeff Malone*	11,083
3	Wes Unseld*	10,624
4	Kevin Loughery*	9,833
5	Gus Johnson*	9,781
6	Phil Chenier*	9,778
7	Walt Bellamy*	9,020
8	Greg Ballard*	8,706
9	Juwan Howard*	8,530
10	Jack Marin*	8,017

N B A . C O M   F U N   F A C T

When Elvin Hayes retired after 16 NBA seasons, he ranked third all time in points scored with 27,313.

79

CHAMPIONSHIP SPURS
There was a state of euphoria in the SBC Center as the San Antonio Spurs celebrated the franchise's second NBA title after defeating the New Jersey Nets in six games in the 2003 NBA Finals.

MR. NBA FINALS

Although he earned the reputation as one of the greatest, if not the greatest, defensive players in NBA history, Bill Russell also knew how to fill it up as well. He ranks fifth all time in points scored during the NBA Finals with 1,151.

THE TOP 10
Highest Scoring Averages†

	PLAYER	G	FGM	FTM	PTS	AVG
1	Rick Barry*	10	138	87	363	36.3
2	Shaquille O'Neal	19	253	144	650	34.2
3	Michael Jordan*	35	438	258	1,176	33.6
4	Jerry West*	55	612	455	1,679	30.5
5	Bob Pettit*	25	241	227	709	28.4
6	Hakeem Olajuwon*	17	187	91	467	27.5
7	Elgin Baylor*	44	442	277	1,161	26.4
8	Tim Duncan	11	105	72	282	25.6
9	Julius Erving*	22	216	128	561	25.5
10	Joe Fulks*	11	84	104	272	24.7

† 10 games minimum

The Top 10 Leading Scorers

Player/Points

1 Jerry West* 1,679 **2** Kareem Abdul-Jabbar* 1,317 **3** Michael Jordan* 1,176 **4** Elgin Baylor* 1,161 **5** Bill Russell* 1,151 **6** Sam Jones* 1,143 **7** Tom Heinsohn* 1,035 **8** John Havlicek* 1,020 **9** Magic Johnson* 971 **10** James Worthy* 754

THE TOP 10
Most Field Goals

	PLAYER	FIELD GOALS
1	Jerry West*	612
2	Kareem Abdul-Jabbar*	544
3	Sam Jones*	458
4	Elgin Baylor*	442
5	Michael Jordan*	438
6	Bill Russell*	415
7	Tom Heinsohn*	407
8	John Havlicek*	390
9	Magic Johnson*	339
10	James Worthy*	314

MR. CLUTCH

During Jerry West's 14 NBA seasons in Los Angeles, the Lakers reached the NBA Finals nine times. West shined in the championship series, winning one MVP award, and he also owns the record for most field-goal attempts with 612.

THE TOP 10
Highest Field-Goal Percentages†

	PLAYER	FGM	FGA	PCT
1	Shaquille O'Neal	253	425	.595
2	John Paxson*	71	120	.592
3	Bill Walton*	74	130	.569
4	Wilt Chamberlain*	264	472	.559
5	Luc Longley*	59	107	.551
6	Kevin McHale*	210	386	.544
7=	Bobby Jones*	77	143	.538
=	Walt Frazier*	129	240	.538
9	James Worthy*	314	589	.533
10	Kurt Rambis*	78	147	.531

† 50 FGM minimum

A key member of the Chicago Bulls in the early 1990s, John Paxson elbowed past many big men to rank second all time in field-goal percentage.

DID YOU KNOW?
Jerry West is the only player in NBA history to win the NBA Finals MVP award as a member of the losing team. He won it in 1969, when Los Angeles lost to the Boston Celtics in seven games.

The Top 10 Most Free Throws

Player/Free Throws

1 Jerry West* 455 **2** Bill Russell* 321 **3** Magic Johnson* 284 **4** Elgin Baylor* 277
5 George Mikan* 259 **6** Michael Jordan* 258 **7** John Havlicek* 240
8 Kareem Abdul-Jabbar* 229 **9** =Sam Jones* 227; =Bob Pettit* 227

THE TOP 10

Highest Free-Throw Percentages†

	PLAYER	FTM	FTA	PCT
1	Reggie Miller	45	46	.978
2	Bill Sharman*	126	136	.926
3	Joe Dumars*	79	89	.888
4	Sam Cassell	45	51	.882
5	Magic Johnson*	284	325	.874
6	Larry Bird*	177	203	.872
7	Paul Seymour*	79	91	.868
8	Terry Porter	68	79	.861
9	Adrian Dantley*	55	64	.859
10	Shawn Kemp	42	49	.857

† 40 FTM minimum

Boston Celtics great Bill Sharman led the NBA in free-throw shooting a record seven times.

THE TOP 10

Highest 3-Pt. Field-Goal Percentages†

	PLAYER	3FGM	3FGA	PCT
1	Glen Rice	12	19	.632
2	Scott Wedman*	10	17	.588
3	Derek Fisher	25	43	.581
4	Rick Fox	17	34	.500
5	John Paxson*	17	36	.472
6	Isiah Thomas*	18	39	.462
7	=B. J. Armstrong	11	24	.458
	=Anfernee Hardaway	11	24	.458
9	=Sam Cassell	14	31	.452
10	Mario Elie*	14	32	.438

† 10 3FGM minimum

THE TOP 10

Most Three-Point Field Goals

	PLAYER	THREE-POINTERS
1	Michael Jordan*	42
2	Robert Horry	38
3	Michael Cooper*	35
4	Scottie Pippen	30
5	=Danny Ainge*	27
	=Toni Kukoc	27
7	Derek Fisher	25
8	Bryon Russell	21
9	Sam Perkins*	20
10	Larry Bird*	19

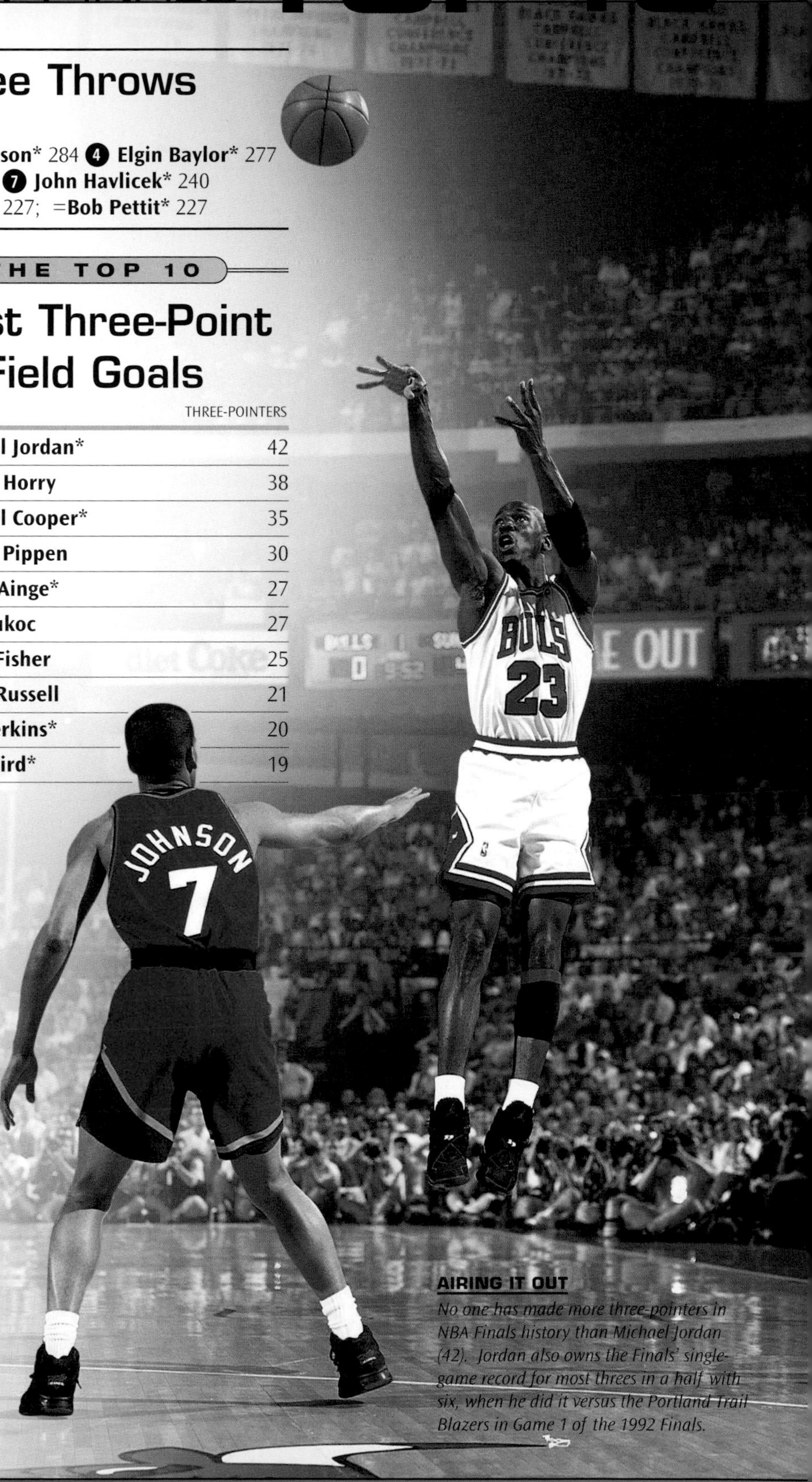

AIRING IT OUT

No one has made more three-pointers in NBA Finals history than Michael Jordan (42). Jordan also owns the Finals' single-game record for most threes in a half with six, when he did it versus the Portland Trail Blazers in Game 1 of the 1992 Finals.

THE TOP 10

Most Games Played

	PLAYER	GAMES
1	Bill Russell*	70
2	Sam Jones*	64
3	Kareem Abdul-Jabbar*	56
4	Jerry West*	55
5	Tom Heinsohn*	52
6	Magic Johnson*	50
7=	John Havlicek*	47
=	Frank Ramsey*	47
9	Michael Cooper*	46
10=	Elgin Baylor*	44
=	K. C. Jones*	44

THE TOP 10

Most Minutes Played

	PLAYER	MINUTES
1	Bill Russell*	3,185
2	Jerry West*	2,375
3	Kareem Abdul-Jabbar*	2,082
4	Magic Johnson*	2,044
5	John Havlicek*	1,872
6	Sam Jones*	1,871
7	Elgin Baylor*	1,850
8	Wilt Chamberlain*	1,657
9	Bob Cousy*	1,639
10	Tom Heinsohn*	1,602

THE TOP 10

Most Defensive Rebounds

	PLAYER	DEFENSIVE REBOUNDS
1	Kareem Abdul-Jabbar*	309
2	Magic Johnson*	308
3	Larry Bird*	282
4	Scottie Pippen	195
5=	Shaquille O'Neal	189
=	Dennis Rodman*	189
7	Robert Parish*	173
8	Paul Silas*	157
9	Michael Jordan*	154
10=	Horace Grant	147
=	Wes Unseld*	147

THE CELTICS' RUNNING MAN

Endurance and durability were only two of the many attributes that made John Havlicek a Hall-of-Fame player. The 6-5 forward/guard starred in 13 consecutive NBA All-Star Games, and was chosen as one of the 50 Greatest Players in NBA History in 1996.

The Top 10 Most Offensive Rebounds

Player/Offensive Rebounds

1 Kareem Abdul-Jabbar* 124 **2** Dennis Rodman* 105 **3** Scottie Pippen 97 **4** =Magic Johnson* 89; =Shaquille O'Neal 89 **6** Robert Parish* 87 **7** Kevin McHale* 85 **8** Larry Bird* 79 **9** Horace Grant 77 **10** Jamaal Wilkes* 74

GLASS CLEANER

A veteran of four NBA Finals, Shaq is hoping to add to his offensive rebounding totals. The three-time NBA Finals MVP currently ranks fourth all time with 89 offensive boards (tied with Magic Johnson).

THE TOP 10
Most Blocked Shots

	PLAYER	BLOCKS
1	Kareem Abdul-Jabbar*	116
2	=Hakeem Olajuwon*	54
	=Shaquille O'Neal	54
	=Robert Parish*	54
5	Kevin McHale*	44
6	Tim Duncan	43
7	Caldwell Jones*	42
8	Julius Erving*	40
9	=Dennis Johnson*	39
	=Scottie Pippen	39

THE TOP 10
Most Rebounds Total

	PLAYER	REBOUNDS
1	Bill Russell*	1,718
2	Wilt Chamberlain*	862
3	Elgin Baylor*	593
4	Kareem Abdul-Jabbar*	507
5	Tom Heinsohn*	473
6	Bob Pettit*	416
7	Magic Johnson*	397
8	Larry Bird*	361
9	John Havlicek*	350
10	Sam Jones*	313

THE TOP 10
Most Steals

	PLAYER	STEALS
1	Magic Johnson*	102
2	Scottie Pippen	67
3	Larry Bird*	63
4	Michael Jordan*	62
5	Michael Cooper*	59
6	Dennis Johnson*	48
7	Danny Ainge*	46
8	Kareem Abdul-Jabbar*	45
9	Julius Erving*	44
10	Robert Horry	41

MAGICAL PLAYER

Magic Johnson played in nine NBA Finals series. The 6-9 guard also owns several finals records, including the highest assist-per-game average with 14.0 (1985) and the highest assist-per-game average by a rookie with 8.7 (1980).

THE TOP 10
Most Assists

	PLAYER	ASSISTS
1	Magic Johnson*	584
2	Bob Cousy*	400
3	Bill Russell*	315
4	Jerry West*	306
5	Dennis Johnson*	228
6	Michael Jordan*	209
7	Scottie Pippen	207
8	John Havlicek*	195
9	Larry Bird*	187
10	Kareem Abdul-Jabbar*	181

NBA.COM FUN FACT

Shaquille O'Neal joined Michael Jordan as the only other player in NBA history to win three NBA Finals MVP awards in a row. The award was first issued in 1969.

85

Most Points

	PLAYER/TEAM	DATE	FG	FT	PTS
1	Elgin Baylor* LAL	4/14/62	22	17	61
2 =Rick Barry* SF		4/18/67	22	11	55
=Michael Jordan* CHI		4/16/93	21	13	55
4	Jerry West* LAL	4/23/69	21	11	53
5	Bob Pettit* STL	4/12/58	19	12	50
6	Allen Iverson PHI	6/6/01	18	9	48
7	Michael Jordan* CHI	6/12/92	14	16	46
8 =Jerry West* LAL		4/19/65	17	11	45
=Jerry West* LAL		4/22/66	19	7	45
=Wilt Chamberlain* LAL		5/6/70	20	5	45
=Michael Jordan* CHI		6/14/98	15	12	45

More than 40 years have passed and no player has eclipsed Elgin Baylor's NBA Finals single-game mark of 61 points. No one other than Baylor has even cracked the 60-point barrier. The 1959 NBA Rookie of the Year set this record in Game 5 of the Finals versus the Boston Celtics. The Lakers defeated the Celtics 126-121 with Baylor accounting for almost 50 percent of his team's total points.

OFFENSIVE FORCE

The NBA's original high flyer, Elgin Baylor averaged 27 points and 12.9 rebounds per game in his 12 seasons with the Lakers. The 11-time All-Star is the Lakers' all-time leading rebounder.

Most Field Goals

	PLAYER/TEAM	DATE	FTM	FTA
1 =Elgin Baylor* LAL		4/14/62	22	46
=Rick Barry* SF		4/18/67	22	48
3 =Jerry West* LAL		4/23/69	21	41
=Michael Jordan* CHI		6/16/93	21	37
=Shaquille O'Neal LAL		6/7/00	21	31
6	Wilt Chamberlain* LAL	5/6/70	20	27
7 =Bob Pettit* STL		4/12/58	19	34
=Jerry West* LAL		4/22/66	19	31
=Kareem Abdul-Jabbar* LAL		5/7/80	19	31
=Michael Jordan* CHI		6/13/93	19	43
=Shaquille O'Neal LAL		6/19/00	19	32

Shaquille O'Neal broke through into the pantheon of NBA greats when he led the Lakers to the 2000 NBA title. He was in the zone the entire series.

Most Free Throws

	PLAYER/TEAM	DATE	FTM	FTA
1	Bob Pettit* STL	4/19/58	19	24
2	Shaquille O'Neal LAL	6/9/00	18	39
3 =Cliff Hagan* STL		3/30/58	17	18
=Elgin Baylor* LAL		4/14/62	17	19
=Jerry West* LAL		4/21/65	17	20
=Jerry West* LAL		4/25/69	17	20
7 =Bob Pettit* STL		4/11/57	16	22
=Michael Jordan* CHI		6/12/92	16	19
9	Many tied with			15

Hall of Famer Bob Pettit made defenses pay whether it was from the field or from the free-throw line. Pettit was rock solid from the charity stripe during the 1958 NBA Finals when the St. Louis Hawks defeated the Boston Celtics.

Most Steals

	PLAYER/TEAM	DATE	STEALS
1	Robert Horry HOU	6/9/95	7
2 =John Havlicek* BOS		5/3/74	6
=Steve Mix* PHI		5/22/77	6
=Maurice Cheeks* PHI		5/7/80	6
=Isiah Thomas* DET		6/19/88	6
6	Many tied with		5

A streaky perimeter shooter, Robert Horry can also excel defensively as well. As a member of the back-to-back 1994 and '95 championship Houston Rockets, Horry picked up seven steals in Game 2 of the 1995 NBA Finals against the Orlando Magic. The 6-10 forward also played in all six games of the 2000 NBA Finals series as a member of the L.A. Lakers, who won against the Indiana Pacers. Now Horry hopes to climb the charts as a San Antonio Spur.

DID YOU KNOW?
Elgin Baylor is currently the Vice President of Basketball Operations for the Los Angeles Clippers, where he has maintained that position since 1986.

HOUDINI OF THE HARDWOOD

Bob Cousy was one of the most creative playmakers in NBA history. The 6-1 guard would mesmerize opponents with his ball-handling and passing skills, dribbling the ball between his legs or passing behind his back. Cousy wowed crowds everywhere he played

THE TOP 10

Most Assists

	PLAYER/TEAM	DATE	ASSISTS
1	Magic Johnson* LAL	6/3/84	21
2=	Magic Johnson* LAL	6/4/87	20
=	Magic Johnson* LAL	6/12/91	20
4=	Bob Cousy* BOS	4/9/57	19
=	Bob Cousy* BOS	4/7/59	19
=	Walt Frazier* NY	5/8/70	19
=	Magic Johnson* LAL	6/14/87	19
=	Magic Johnson* LAL	6/19/88	19
9	Jerry West* LAL	5/1/70	18
10=	Magic Johnson* LAL	6/6/84	17
=	Dennis Johnson* BOS	6/7/85	17
=	Magic Johnson* LAL	6/7/85	17
=	Robert Reid* HOU	6/5/86	17
=	Magic Johnson* LAL	6/16/88	17

THE TOP 10

Most Blocked Shots

	PLAYER/TEAM	DATE	BLOCKS
1=	Bill Walton* POR	6/5/77	8
=	Hakeem Olajuwon* HOU	6/5/86	8
=	Patrick Ewing* NY	6/17/94	8
=	Shaquille O'Neal LAL	6/8/01	8
=	Tim Duncan SAN	6/15/03	8
6=	Dennis Johnson* SEA	5/28/78	7
=	Patrick Ewing* NY	6/12/94	7
=	Hakeem Olajuwon* HOU	6/12/94	7
9=	Kareem Abdul-Jabbar* LAL	5/4/80	6
=	Patrick Ewing* NY	6/10/94	6

DENIED!

Tim Duncan of the San Antonio Spurs put on a defensive clinic in the 2003 NBA Finals. The 7-0 forward/center was an imposing defensive force that limited the New Jersey Nets' ability to score near the hoop.

THE TOP 10

Most Rebounds

	PLAYER/TEAM	DATE	REB.
1=	Bill Russell* BOS	3/29/60	40
=	Bill Russell* BOS	4/18/62	40
3=	Bill Russell* BOS	4/11/61	38
=	Bill Russell* BOS	4/16/63	38
=	Wilt Chamberlain* SF	4/24/64	38
=	Wilt Chamberlain* PHI	4/16/67	38
7	Bill Russell* BOS	4/9/60	35
8	Wilt Chamberlain* PHI	4/14/67	33
9=	Bill Russell* BOS	4/13/57	32
=	Bill Russell* BOS	4/22/64	32
=	Bill Russell* BOS	4/28/66	32

All-Time Series Records

	TEAM	W/L	PCT
1=	**Chicago Bulls**	6/0	1.000
=	**San Antonio Spurs**	2/0	1.000
=	**Baltimore Bullets***	1/0	1.000
=	**Sacramento Kings**	1/0	1.000
5	**Boston Celtics**	16/3	.842
6	**Los Angeles Lakers**	14/13	.519
7=	**Golden State Warriors**	3/3	.500
=	**Houston Rockets**	2/2	.500
=	**Milwaukee Bucks**	1/1	.500
10	**Detroit Pistons**	2/3	.400

The Boston Celtics may own the most NBA titles with 16 but the Lakers franchise owns the record for most NBA Finals appearances with 27. Dating back to when they played in Minneapolis, the Lakers won five titles in six years before suffering a drought after the team moved to Los Angeles in 1960. During a nine-year period, the franchise made seven Finals appearances and came home empty every time. The Lakers finally broke through in 1972, when they defeated the New York Knicks in six games.

CHAMPIONSHIP DUO

Two of the NBA's greatest players—Tim Duncan and David Robinson—led the San Antonio Spurs to two titles in five years. Robinson proved to be the ultimate teammate, deferring to Duncan, who won NBA Finals MVP honors both times.

Games Won/Lost Percentage

	TEAM	W/L	PCT
1	**San Antonio Spurs**	8/3	.727
2	**Chicago Bulls**	24/11	.686
3	**Baltimore Bullets***	4/2	.667
4	**Milwaukee Bucks**	7/4	.636
5	**Boston Celtics**	70/46	.603
6	**Sacramento Kings**	4/3	.571
7	**Golden State Warriors**	17/14	.548
8	**Detroit Pistons**	15/13	.536
9	**Houston Rockets**	12/11	.522
10=	**Los Angeles Lakers**	78/78	.500
=	**Seattle SuperSonics**	9/9	.500

The Houston Rockets participated in four NBA Finals in a 15-year span. The Boston Celtics defeated the Rockets in the 1981 and 1986 Finals, while Houston won back-to-back titles in the mid-1990s. Hakeem Olajuwon cemented his status as one of the greatest centers to ever play the game when he led the Rockets to championship wins over the New York Knicks in 1994, and the Orlando Magic in 1995.

THE 1964–65 BOSTON CELTICS

"Win one for Walter" was the overwhelming sentiment among every one of the Boston Celtics as the 1964–65 season was set to begin. The Celtics' owner and founder, Walter Brown, had recently passed away and the players' championship mission now had a much clearer focus.

The Celtics ran off 11 consecutive wins to start the season and finished with a NBA-best 62 wins, 14 ahead of the second-place Cincinnati Royals in the Eastern Division. Boston did it with defense, allowing only 104.5 points per game while averaging 112.8. Bill Russell once again led the defensive attack, averaging 24.5 rebounds per game. The Celtics' roll almost came to an end in the playoffs as they were challenged in the Eastern Division Finals by the Philadelphia 76ers. In the remaining seconds of Game 7, Boston clung to a 110-109 lead until John Havlicek brilliantly stole the ball from Hal Greer to secure the win.

THE TOP 10

First NBA Champions

YEAR	TEAM
1947	Philadelphia Warriors*
1948	Baltimore Bullets*
1949	Minneapolis Lakers*
1950	Minneapolis Lakers*
1951	Rochester Royals*
1952	Minneapolis Lakers*
1953	Minneapolis Lakers*
1954	Minneapolis Lakers*
1955	Syracuse Nationals*
1956	Philadelphia Warriors*

CHAMPIONSHIP CENTER

George Mikan was the main reason the Minneapolis Lakers established themselves as the NBA's first dynasty. Mikan led the Lakers to five NBA titles in six years, including three in a row.

THE TOP 10

Last NBA Champions

YEAR	TEAM
2003	San Antonio Spurs
2002	Los Angeles Lakers
2001	Los Angeles Lakers
2000	Los Angeles Lakers
1999	San Antonio Spurs
1998	Chicago Bulls
1997	Chicago Bulls
1996	Chicago Bulls
1995	Houston Rockets
1994	Houston Rockets

Multiple-championship teams have been in vogue for the last 10 seasons. Chicago continued the trend of the late 1980s, when the Lakers and Pistons won back-to-back titles. The Bulls turned it up a notch by winning three in a row on two separate occasions (1991–93 and 1996–98).

THE TOP 10

All-Time Home Records

	TEAM	W/L	PCT
1	Baltimore Bullets*	3/0	1.000
2	San Antonio Spurs	4/1	.800
3=	Detroit Pistons	9/3	.750
=	Golden State Warriors	12/4	.750
=	Sacramento Kings	3/1	.750
6	Boston Celtics	44/17	.721
7	Chicago Bulls	12/5	.706
8=	Houston Rockets	8/4	.667
=	Indiana Pacers	2/1	.667
=	Seattle SuperSonics	6/3	.667
=	Washington Capitols*	2/1	.667

In 1999, the San Antonio Spurs became the first former ABA team to win an NBA championship. The Spurs won their second title four years later.

THE TOP 10

All-Time Road Records

	TEAM	W/L	PCT
1	Milwaukee Bucks	4/1	.800
2=	Chicago Bulls	12/6	.667
=	San Antonio Spurs	4/2	.667
4	Boston Celtics	26/29	.473
5	Los Angeles Lakers	32/46	.410
6=	Detroit Pistons	6/10	.375
=	Portland Trail Blazers	3/5	.375
8	Houston Rockets	4/7	.364
9=	Baltimore Bullets*	1/2	.333
=	Golden State Warriors	5/10	.333
=	Phoenix Suns	2/4	.333
=	Sacramento Kings	1/2	.333
=	Seattle SuperSonics	3/6	.333

The Chicago Bulls clinched three of their six NBA titles on the road in the 1990s. The ability to close out a team on the road is a difficult and challenging feat.

INDEX

CREDITS

PHOTO CREDITS

1 Jesse D. Garrabrant

2-3 Dick Raphael; Jaime Squire

4-5 Steve Nash: Glenn James; George Mikan: NBA Photos; Magic Johnson: Nathaniel S. Butler; Tim Duncan: Andrew D. Bernstein

6-7 Andrew D. Bernstein; Ron Hoskins

8-9 Nathanial S. Butler

10-11 Tim Duncan: Andrew D. Bernstein; Michael Jordan: Jonathan Daniel; Don Nelson: Jed Jacobsohn; Pat Riley: Victor Baldizon

12-13 Karl Malone: NBA Photos; Ray Allen: Garrett Ellwood; Steve Nash: Glenn James

14-15 Horace Grant: Jeff Gross; Charles Oakley: Nathaniel S. Butler; Dikembe Mutombo: Noah Graham

16-17 Kareem Abdul-Jabbar: Tim DeFrisco; Allen Iverson: Gary Bassing; Reggie Miller: Ron Hoskins

18-19 Charles Barkley: Mike Powell; Wilt Chamberlain: NBA Photos; Michael Jordan: Nathaniel S. Butler; Isiah Thomas: Otto Greule Jr.

20-21 Wilt Chamberlain: Dick Raphael; Scott Skiles: Tom Smart; Mark Eaton: Mike Powell

22-23 Calvin Murphy: NBA Photos; Artis Gilmore: Bill Baptist; John Stockton: Mike Moore

24-25 Red Auerbach: Greg Foster; Bill Walton: NBA Photos; Julius Erving: Andrew D. Bernstein

26-27 Lenny Wilkens: Ron Turenne; Phil Jackson: Andrew D. Bernstein; Red Auerbach: Getty Images

28-29 Los Angeles Lakers: NBA Photos; Phil Jackson: Andrew D. Bernstein; A. C. Green: David Taylor

30-31 Mark Eaton: Tim DeFrisco; Ben Wallace: Tom Pidgeon; Bill Russell: Dick Raphael

32-33 Dikembe Mutombo: Noren Trotman; Hakeem Olajuwon: Stephen Dunn; Vlade Divac: Rocky Widner

34-35 Bill Bradley: Neil Leifer; Yao Ming: Jesse D. Garrabrant; Kareem Abdul-Jabbar: Walter Iooss Jr.

36-37 Bob Cousy: NBA Photos; Magic Johnson: Nathaniel S. Butler; Jason Kidd: Jamie Squire

38-39 Allen Iverson: Scott Cunningham; Michael Jordan: Nathaniel S. Butler; Jerry Lucas: NBA Photos

40-41 Dominique Wilkins: Mike Powell; Bob Pettit: NBA Photos; Kevin Garnett: Jennifer Pottheiser

42-43 Brent Barry: Layne Murdoch; Rick Barry: NBA Photos; Manute Bol: Tim DeFrisco; Muggsy Bogues: Steve Grayson

44-45 Chicago Bulls: Scott Cunningham; Hall of Fame: Naismith Memorial Basketball Hall of Fame

46-47 Walter Iooss Jr.

48-49 Paul Pierce: Jesse D. Garrabrant; Shaquille O'Neal: Andrew D. Bernstein; Predrag Stojakovic: Rocky Widner

50-51 Scottie Pippen: Jonathan Daniel; Horace Grant: Donald Miralle; Gary Payton: Ezra Shaw

52-53 Allen Iverson: Jesse D. Garrabrant; Kevin McHale: NBA Photos; Mark Price: Nathaniel S. Butler

54-55 Kareem Abdul-Jabbar: Mike Powell; Larry Bird: Walter Iooss Jr.; Hakeem Olajuwon: Bill Baptist

56-57 Rick Barry: Ronald Modra; Magic Johnson: Ken Levine

58-59 Team photos: NBA Photos; Boston Garden: Andrew D. Bernstein

60-61 Chuck Daly: Jonathan Daniel; Pat Riley: Victor Baldizon; Kobe/Phil Jackson/Shaq: Andrew D. Bernstein

62-63 NBA Photos

64-65 Steve Smith: Getty Images; Steve Nash: Glenn James; Richard Hamilton: Nathaniel S. Butler

66-67 Hakeem Olajuwon: NBAE Photos; Tim Hardaway: Eliot J. Schechter; Toni Kukoc: Jesse D. Garrabrant

68-69 Patrick Ewing: Nathaniel S. Butler; Anfernee Hardaway: Barry Gossage; Dan Majerle: Stephen Dunn

70-71 San Antonio Spurs: Nathaniel S. Butler; Detlef Schrempf: Stephen Dunn; Utah Jazz: Kent Horner

72-73 John Havlicek: Ken Regan; Jerry Sloan: Brian Bahr; Alex English: NBA Photos

74-75 Calvin Murphy: Jim Cummins; Glen Rice: Nathaniel S. Butler

76-77 Walt Frazier: Jim Cummins; Buck Williams: Noren Trotman; Hal Greer: George Kalinsky

78-79 David Robinson: Andrew D. Bernstein; Oscar Robertson and Elvin Hayes: Walter Iooss Jr.

80-81 Nathaniel S. Butler

82-83 Bill Russell and Jerry West: NBA Photos; Michael Jordan: Nathaniel S. Butler

84-85 John Havlicek: Dick Raphael; Shaquille O'Neal: Ezra Shaw; Magic Johnson: Mike Powell

86-87 Elgin Baylor: Wen Roberts; Bob Cousy: NBA Photos; Tim Duncan: Andrew D. Bernstein

88-89 Duncan/Robinson: Jesse D. Garrabrant; Boston Celtics and George Mikan: NBA Photos

ACKNOWLEDGMENTS

A deviation from The Top 10 list format is required when it comes to praising the efforts of all of those involved in completing this project. A full slate of No. 1's is assigned to those who consistently reached championship-level heights. The point guard and captain on this project—Anja Schmidt of DK—flawlessly managed the details and editing of this project. The DK team of Megan Clayton, Michelle Baxter, Dirk Kaufman, Tina Vaughan, and Sharon Lucas, elegantly and brilliantly pulled the whole project together. At the NBA, Charles Rosenzweig, Joe Amati, Michael Levine, Margaret Williams, Scott Yurdin, Brian Choi, and Mario Argote provided the neccessary support to achieve peak results. Rounding out this publishing Dream Team is Steve Hirdt, Chris Thorn, and Santo Labombarda at Elias Sports Bureau, who supplied the statistical information, guidance, and fun.—JH